SNAP
REVISION

THE MERCHANT OF VENICE

AQA GCSE English Literature

PAUL
BURNS

REVISE SET TEXTS IN A SNAP

C000025326

Published by Collins
An imprint of HarperCollinsPublishers
1 London Bridge Street,
London, SE1 9GF

© HarperCollinsPublishers Limited 2017

9780008247096

First published 2017

10 9 8 7 6 5 4 3 2 1

British Library Cataloguing in Publication Data.

A CIP record of this book is available from the
British Library.

Printed in the UK by Martins the Printer Ltd.

Commissioning Editor: Gillian Bowman
Managing Editor: Craig Balfour
Author: Paul Burns
Copyeditor: David Christie
Proofreaders: Jill Laidlaw and Louise Robb
Project management and typesetting:
  Mark Steward
Cover designers: Kneath Associates and
  Sarah Duxbury
Production: Natalia Rebow

ACKNOWLEDGEMENTS

The author and publisher are grateful to the
copyright holders for permission to use quoted
materials and images.

Every effort has been made to trace copyright
holders and obtain their permission for the use of
copyright material. The author and publisher will
gladly receive information enabling them to rectify
any error or omission in subsequent editions. All
facts are correct at time of going to press.

Contents

Act 1

You must be able to: understand what happens at the beginning of the play.

What is the setting?

Scenes 1 and 3 are set in Venice. Scene 2 is set in Belmont, where Portia lives.

What do we learn in scene 1?

The merchant, Antonio, tells his friends he feels sad but does not know why. His ships are trading abroad but he says he is not worried about his investments as he has not put all his money into one venture.

Bassanio, Antonio's **kinsman**, wants to borrow money from Antonio. He has spent all his own money and has been helped by Antonio in the past. He knows a beautiful **heiress**, Portia, and he wants money so that he can court her.

Antonio says he does not have any money available to lend but he will borrow money, which he will then lend to Bassanio.

What do we learn in scene 2?

At Belmont, Portia discusses her situation with her waiting-woman, Nerissa. Before his death, her father decided that she should not be able to choose who to marry. Instead he left three chests – one of gold, one of silver and one of lead. Any man who wants to marry Portia must choose between them. If he chooses the right one, she must marry him.

They talk about various **suitors** who have come to Belmont. None of them wants to choose between the caskets, which pleases Portia. Nerissa remembers Bassanio and Portia agrees that he is 'deserving'.

At the end of the scene, a servant tells Portia that a new suitor, the Prince of Morocco, has arrived.

What happens in scene 3?

In Venice, Bassanio meets Shylock who agrees to lend him 3,000 ducats for three months on Antonio's **bond**.

As Antonio approaches, Shylock reveals to the audience that he hates him because he is a Christian and because he lends money without charging interest. He also says that Antonio hates Jews.

Shylock tells Antonio a story from the Bible about **Jacob**. They disagree about whether it means charging interest is permissible.

Shylock asks why, when he hates him and treats him badly, Antonio should expect Shylock to lend him money. Antonio replies that if he does not pay it back he is willing to pay a penalty.

Shylock says that, out of kindness, and as 'a merry sport', he will make the penalty for non-payment of the debt a pound of Antonio's flesh. Antonio agrees.

Bassanio: 'In Belmont is a lady richly left,' (Ii)

Nerissa: 'He, of all the men that ever my foolish eyes looked upon, was the best deserving a fair lady.' (Iii)

Shylock: 'Three thousand ducats for three months, and Antonio bound.' (Iiii)

Summary

- Bassanio asks Antonio to lend him money so that he can go to Belmont to ask Portia to marry him.
- Antonio agrees but says all his money is tied up and he will have to borrow.
- Portia's suitors must choose between three chests. The man who chooses the right chest can marry Portia.
- Shylock lends Bassanio 3,000 ducats on Antonio's bond.
- If Antonio does not repay him on time he will have to give Shylock a pound of flesh.

Questions

QUICK TEST
1. In which two places is the first act set?
2. Why does Bassanio want to borrow money?
3. What do Antonio and Shylock disagree about?
4. What will Shylock take if Antonio does not repay him?

EXAM PRACTICE
Using at least one of the 'Key Quotations to Learn', write a paragraph explaining how Shakespeare sets the scene for the rest of the play in Act 1.

You must be able to: understand what happens in Act 2.

What happens in scene 1?

In Belmont, the Prince of Morocco tells Portia that he will choose between the caskets. He agrees to a condition set by Portia's father: if he chooses the wrong one he will never marry.

What happens in Venice in scene 2?

Launcelot Gobbo, Shylock's servant, debates with himself whether he should run away. He is approached by an old, partly blind man, who asks him the way to Shylock's house. Launcelot recognises his father and pretends for a while that he is not Launcelot, before revealing his identity.

He tells his father that he wants to leave Shylock to serve Bassanio. When Bassanio enters, he agrees to employ Launcelot.

Bassanio also agrees to Gratiano's request to go with him to Belmont, but makes him promise to behave more sensibly. He says he will see him later at a dinner he is giving before his departure.

What does Jessica do in scene 3?

Shylock's daughter, Jessica, says goodbye to Launcelot and gives him a letter to pass on to Lorenzo. She vows that she will become a Christian and marry Lorenzo.

What happens in scene 4?

Gratiano, Lorenzo and their friends are planning to leave Bassanio's dinner and dress up for a **masque** when Launcelot arrives with the letter. In the letter, Jessica tells him to come to her father's house and she will elope with him.

What does Shylock do in scene 5?

As he leaves to go to Bassanio's dinner, Shylock tells Jessica to lock the doors and not let in the **masquers** that Launcelot has told him to expect.

What happens in scene 6?

Jessica, dressed as a page boy, leaves Shylock's house with Lorenzo and a casket of her father's jewels and money. Antonio tells Gratiano that Bassanio is about to set sail.

What happens in Belmont in scene 7?

In Belmont, the Prince of Morocco chooses the golden casket. Inside there is a '**carrion death**' and a scroll that tells him 'All that glisters is not gold'. He leaves.

What happens in Venice in scene 8?

Salerio and Solanio talk about Lorenzo and Jessica's **elopement**. Shylock has been seen in the streets shouting about his daughter and his ducats.

What happens in Belmont in scene 9?

A new suitor, the Prince of Arragon, has arrived. He chooses the silver casket and finds a 'blinking idiot' inside. After he has gone, a messenger tells Portia that a young Venetian has arrived.

Key Quotations to Learn

Jessica: 'Farewell; and if my fortune be not crost, / I have a father, you a daughter, lost.' (IIiii)

Shylock: 'What, are there masques? Hear you me, Jessica: / Lock up my doors;' (IIv)

Solanio: 'Let good Antonio look he keep his day / Or he shall pay for this.' (IIviii)

Summary

- Launcelot Gobbo, Shylock's servant, leaves him and goes to work for Bassanio.
- Lorenzo elopes with Jessica, Shylock's daughter.
- The Prince of Morocco and the Prince of Arragon choose the wrong caskets.
- Bassanio sails to Belmont.

Questions

QUICK TEST
1. What two things does Jessica vow to do?
2. What does Jessica disguise herself as?
3. Which casket does the Prince of Morocco choose?
4. Which casket does the Prince of Arragon choose?

EXAM PRACTICE
Using at least one of the 'Key Quotations to Learn', write a paragraph explaining how Shakespeare builds tension and a sense of anticipation in Act 2.

Act 3

You must be able to: understand what happens in Act 3.

What happens in scene 1?

Salerio tells Solanio that one of Antonio's ships has been lost. Shylock accuses them of knowing about Jessica's elopement. They admit it. He tells them that if Antonio cannot pay him back, he will ask for his bond.

Tubal, a Jewish friend of Shylock, comes with the news that Jessica has been seen spending his money and swapping a ring for a monkey. He also tells him that another of Antonio's 'argosies' has been wrecked. Shylock is pleased to hear of Antonio's bad luck and is determined to pursue him for his bond.

How do things change in scene 2?

In Belmont, Portia tries to persuade Bassanio not to choose a casket because she does not want to lose him. He says he does not want any more 'torture'. They are in love. Bassanio chooses the lead casket and finds a portrait of Portia in it.

She says she will marry him and give him all her wealth. She gives him a ring as a token of love, which she says he must not part with. He swears that the ring will not leave his finger until he is dead.

Nerissa and Gratiano reveal that they have fallen in love and intend to marry.

Salerio arrives with Lorenzo and Jessica, whom he has met on the way, and a letter from Antonio. In it, he says he cannot pay his debt to Shylock and asks Bassanio to return to Venice. Portia says he must go and pay whatever it takes to save Antonio.

What happens in scene 3?

In Venice, Antonio is being taken to gaol. Shylock refuses to listen to his pleas.

What happens in Belmont in scene 4?

Portia puts Lorenzo and Jessica in charge of her house, saying that she and Nerissa are going to live a life of prayer in a monastery until the return of their husbands.

She then sends a servant to Padua to get 'notes and garments' from a cousin, Dr Bellario, who is a doctor of law there. She tells Nerissa that the two of them are going to Venice disguised as men.

Key Quotations to Learn

Bassanio: 'What find I here? / Fair Portia's counterfeit!' (IIIii)

Portia: 'This house, these servants, and this same myself / Are yours, my lord. I give them with this ring;' (IIIii)

Shylock: 'I'll have my bond. I will not hear thee speak;' (IIIiii)

Summary

- Antonio loses his ships and Shylock decides he wants his bond.
- Bassanio chooses the correct casket – the one made of lead – and Portia agrees to marry him.
- Nerissa and Gratiano agree to marry.
- After hearing Antonio's news, Bassanio and Gratiano return to Venice.
- Portia and Nerissa plan to disguise themselves as men and go to Venice.

Questions

QUICK TEST
1. How does Shylock react to Antonio's bad luck?
2. Which casket does Bassanio choose?
3. What does Portia give Bassanio as a **symbol** of their love?
4. Who is left in charge of Belmont?

EXAM PRACTICE
Using at least one of the 'Key Quotations to Learn', write a paragraph explaining the consequences of the loss of Antonio's ships for the other characters.

Act 4

You must be able to: understand what happens in Act 4.

How does Act 4 scene 1 start?

The scene is Antonio's trial, presided over by the Duke of Venice.

The Duke asks Shylock to have pity on Antonio. He refuses, saying he has sworn to have his bond. He says he cannot explain why except that he hates Antonio.

Bassanio offers Shylock twice the amount of the debt but Shylock refuses. The Duke asks how he can hope for mercy if he does not give it. Shylock replies that he does not fear judgment because he has done nothing wrong: by law, the pound of flesh is his.

How do things change?

The Duke is waiting for legal opinion from Dr Bellario. Nerissa, disguised as a legal clerk, brings him a letter. Shylock sharpens his knife on the sole of his shoe. The letter says that Bellario is sick and has sent a 'young and learned doctor' called Balthasar.

Portia enters disguised as Balthasar.

What is Portia's argument?

Portia asks Shylock to show mercy but he again refuses. Bassanio offers to pay more than the money owed but Portia says that, as Shylock refuses to accept it, Antonio must give his pound of flesh.

Portia tells Shylock that he must take exactly a pound of flesh. However, he must take no blood. If he sheds even a drop of blood, Venetian law says that all his land and goods will be confiscated.

What are the consequences for Shylock?

Shylock now says he will take Bassanio's offer but Portia says he cannot. She also tells the court that, according to the law, if an **alien** seeks to kill a Venetian citizen, the victim can seize half his property and the other half must go to the state.

The Duke says he will spare Shylock's life and take a fine instead of half his goods. Antonio says he wants his half to be put 'in use' or **trust** until Shylock's death, after which, it is to go to Jessica and Lorenzo. He will only do this on condition that Shylock becomes a Christian.

Shylock agrees and leaves the court, saying he is unwell.

What happens at the end of Act 4 scene 1?

Bassanio offers to pay Portia, who is still disguised as Balthasar, but she refuses. She agrees to take his gloves. She then asks for his ring. He refuses to give it to her, explaining that his wife has made him swear never to sell it, lose it or give it away.

However, when Portia has left, Antonio persuades Bassanio to give her the ring.

What happens in scene 2?

Portia is sending Nerissa to Shylock's house with a deed to sign when Gratiano arrives with Bassanio's ring. Nerissa tells Portia she will try to get her ring from Gratiano.

Key Quotations to Learn

Bassanio: 'Why dost thou whet thy knife so earnestly?' (IVi)

Shylock: 'My deeds upon my head! I crave the law, / The penalty and forfeit of my bond.' (IVi)

Portia: 'The Jew shall have all justice. Soft, no haste, / He shall have nothing but the penalty.' (IVi)

Summary

- Shylock refuses to have mercy on Antonio or accept Bassanio's offer of money.
- Portia says Shylock can take exactly a pound of flesh but he must not take a drop of blood.
- Shylock does not take the flesh.
- Because he has tried to kill a Venetian, all Shylock's property can be confiscated, half going to the state and half to Antonio.
- Antonio says he will take his half 'in use' for Jessica and Lorenzo, provided Shylock becomes a Christian. Shylock agrees.
- Portia asks Bassanio for his ring instead of a fee. Antonio persuades him to give it to her.

Questions

QUICK TEST
1. What reason does Shylock give for not showing mercy to Antonio?
2. Who is Balthasar?
3. Who will get Shylock's property when he dies?

EXAM PRACTICE
Using at least one of the 'Key Quotations to Learn', write a paragraph explaining how Shakespeare creates dramatic tension in Act 4 scene 1.

Act 5

You must be able to: understand what happens at the end of the play.

How does Act 5 start?

In Belmont at night, Lorenzo and Jessica talk about classical stories of tragic lovers and about their own love. News is brought that both Portia and Bassanio are on their way home. Lorenzo asks for music to be played while they wait for them.

Portia and Nerissa return. Shortly afterwards, Bassanio arrives with Gratiano and Antonio. Portia welcomes Antonio.

What happens next?

Nerissa quarrels with Gratiano because he has given away his ring. He protests that he gave it to the 'clerk' and not to a woman. She says she does not believe him. Portia says that her husband would never give away the ring she gave him.

Gratiano tells her that Bassanio gave his ring to 'Balthasar'. He admits it but Portia says she believes he gave it to a woman. He defends his actions but Portia replies that if ever she sees the lawyer she will sleep with him. Nerissa says she will sleep with the clerk.

Antonio begs their pardon and says it is his fault and, when Bassanio swears he will never break another oath, says he will be his surety.

Portia gives a ring to Antonio and tells him to give it to Bassanio. He recognises it and she tells him she got it from the young **doctor** when he 'lay with' her. Nerissa produces her own ring, which she says she got from the clerk.

How does the play end?

Portia explains everything to the shocked men. She also tells Antonio that she has news of some of his ships returning. Nerissa gives Jessica and Lorenzo the deed that Shylock has made in their favour.

The play ends with the married couples reconciled.

Key Quotations to Learn

Lorenzo: 'In such a night as this,' (Vi)

Portia: 'How far that little candle throws his beams! / So shines a good deed in a naughty world!' (Vi)

Antonio: 'I am th'unhappy subject of these quarrels.' (Vi)

Summary

- Portia and Nerissa accuse their husbands of giving away their rings to women.
- Bassanio and Gratiano say they gave them to the young doctor and his clerk.
- Bassanio says that if she forgives him he will never break an oath again.
- Portia and Nerissa produce the rings and say that they got them from the doctor and his clerk.
- Portia then reveals that she and Nerissa were Balthasar and his clerk.

Questions

QUICK TEST
1. What are Lorenzo and Jessica talking about when the scene opens?
2. Where and when is the final act set?
3. What does Portia give to Antonio to give to Bassanio?
4. What good news does Portia have for Antonio?

EXAM PRACTICE
Using at least one of the 'Key Quotations to Learn', write a paragraph exploring how Shakespeare resolves matters at the end of the play.

Venice and Belmont

You must be able to: understand the **significance** of the play's settings.

Where are Venice and Belmont?

Venice is a real city in modern-day Italy. Belmont is an invented place, probably not very far from Venice.

What was Venice like when Shakespeare wrote *The Merchant of Venice*?

The Merchant of Venice was written around 1597 to 1598, towards the end of the reign of Elizabeth I.

Venice was an independent republic, ruled by the Doge, who was elected for life by the Great Council, which was made up of men from the 'noble families' of the city. They also elected a senate, that ruled with the Doge.

Venice was one of the most powerful **city-states** in the world. It was a centre for trade, especially with Asia, which made it very rich. It also controlled land in Italy and beyond.

Because of its status as a trading nation, Venice was home to many people from other countries. Compared with other states, it was quite tolerant of different religions and ideas.

Why did Shakespeare set the play in Venice?

Shakespeare probably never went to Venice but his work was influenced by Italian writers and he certainly would have known about the city.

The Italian story on which Shakespeare based his plot is not set in Venice. However, the city's reputation as a wealthy trading centre, with a well-established Jewish community, makes it an ideal setting for Shakespeare's characters and themes.

How is the real Venice reflected in the play?

There are several references that 'place' the play in Venice. The Rialto is a real place, there is a reference to the traghetto or ferry (called the 'traject' in the play) and the trial is presided over by the Duke (a translation of Doge).

The main characters reflect the kind of people who might have lived there. Bassanio is a scholar and soldier from a wealthy family, Antonio is a rich merchant and Shylock is a moneylender.

Jewish people were encouraged to live in Venice partly because they could lend money at interest, something that Christians were forbidden to do. This was useful to merchants. Jewish people could worship freely but led quite separate lives from people in the rest of the city.

The place where Jewish people lived is called the Ghetto. They were not allowed to leave the ghetto between 6 p.m. and noon the next day. As Shylock goes to dinner with Christians in the evening, Shakespeare either did not know or chose to ignore this fact.

What is the significance of Belmont?

Shakespeare took the name Belmont from his main source, an Italian story about a lady, who lived at a place called Belmont, the man who wants to marry her, a merchant, and a Jew.

Shakespeare makes Belmont into a romantic place, like somewhere out of a fairy tale. Its quiet, settled **atmosphere** forms a contrast with the busy and risky life of Venice.

Summary

- The play is set in the real city of Venice and the fictional Belmont, where Portia's house is located.
- Venice was an important trading power in the sixteenth century.
- The characters resemble the kind of people who might have lived there.
- Venice was home to a large Jewish community, who lived in the Ghetto.
- The tranquil atmosphere of Belmont contrasts with the busy atmosphere of Venice.

Questions

QUICK TEST
1. Who was the elected ruler of Venice?
2. With which part of the world did Venetians chiefly trade?
3. What were Jews allowed to do that Christians could not?
4. Whose home is at Belmont?

EXAM PRACTICE
Lorenzo: How sweet the moonlight sleeps upon this bank!
             Here we will sit and let the sounds of music
             Creep in our ears; soft stillness and the night
             Become the touches of sweet harmony. (Vi)

Write a paragraph about the atmosphere Shakespeare creates in Belmont and how he creates it.

Christians and Jews in Elizabethan England

You must be able to: understand how **attitudes** in the play and towards the play have been shaped by the context in which it was written

Was England a Christian country in the sixteenth century?

England was a Christian country. Very few people belonged to non-Christian religions or had no religion.

The **established church** was the Church of England but this had not been the case for long. Many people still followed the 'old religion' of Roman Catholicism.

Although Elizabeth I was more tolerant of other Christians than some monarchs and governments, it was illegal not to attend church in the established church at least once a month.

What do Christians believe?

Christians believe that there is one God who made the world and that God sent his son, Jesus Christ, to save us.

Christians believe that mankind was in a state of sin and that Christ's death 'redeemed' us, meaning that our sins can be forgiven and that after death we can join God in Heaven.

Elizabethan Christians would have believed that non-Christians could not achieve Heaven without being converted to Christianity.

Christian morality is based on the Ten Commandments, given to **Moses** in the Old Testament, and the teachings of Christ in the New Testament of the Bible.

Was there a Jewish community in Elizabethan England?

There were very few (probably no more than 200) Jewish people in Elizabethan England, mainly in London. Most of these Jews were Spanish or Portuguese in origin and were (officially at least) converts to Christianity. However, some of them did practise the Jewish faith in private.

Jews had been banished from England by King Edward I in 1290. They were not allowed to return until 1657.

Because of this, very few English people would ever have met a Jew. Their ideas about Jewish beliefs and customs often came from sensational stories about crimes Jews had supposedly committed and strange, witchcraft-like practices that bore no relation to real Jewish customs.

What do Jews believe?

Like Christians, Jews believe in one eternal God, to whom they pray. They believe that God has spoken through the prophets, the greatest of whom was Moses.

Like Christians, they believe that after death God will punish the evil and reward the good.

Their Holy Book is the Torah, which comprises the first five books of the Bible.

They believe that a Messiah (or saviour) will come one day and that the dead will be resurrected. Christians believe that Jesus Christ is the Messiah.

How is this reflected in *The Merchant of Venice*?

The play reflects the position of Jews in Venice rather than in England, as they are a significant part of the Venetian community and can be open about their faith. However, Shylock also suffers because of **anti-Semitism**, especially from Antonio.

As in most of Europe at the time, everyone else is assumed to be Christian. In Venice, most people would have been Catholics but the Christian beliefs referred to in the play would have been shared by members of the Church of England.

Summary

- Elizabethan England was overwhelmingly Christian.
- Jewish people had not been allowed to practise their religion in England since 1290.
- Many English people believed false, and sometimes very strange, things about Jews.
- Jews and Christians all believe in and pray to one, eternal God.
- Jewish life in the play reflects life in Venice more than life in England.

Questions

QUICK TEST
1. How many Jewish people were there in England when Shakespeare was writing?
2. Who followed the 'old religion'?
3. What is the Jewish holy book called?
4. To which religion do most of the characters in *The Merchant of Venice* belong?

EXAM PRACTICE
Relating your ideas to the historical context, write a paragraph explaining how Shakespeare portrays the position of Jews in Venice in *The Merchant of Venice*.

Shakespeare and the Elizabethan Theatre

You must be able to: understand the context in which the play was written and performed.

Who was William Shakespeare?

William Shakespeare (1564–1616) came from a middle-class family in Stratford-upon-Avon and attended the local grammar school.

He lived during a time of increasing prosperity and creativity in England.

Shakespeare became an actor and writer in London. By the time *The Merchant of Venice* was written, he was recognised as one of the leading playwrights of his time.

Where and when was *The Merchant of Venice* first performed?

The Merchant of Venice was first performed in 1596 or 1597 by a company called The Lord Chamberlain's Men, of which Shakespeare was a leading member, in either The Theatre or The Curtain. Later, it would have been performed at The Globe, which was built in 1599.

What was the Elizabethan theatre like?

These theatres, known as 'public theatres', were large buildings with stages that extended into the audience (thrust stages). At the back of the stage there were several entrances and a recessed area and balconies. The stage and part of the audience, which sat in galleries around the side, were covered. The central area, where poorer audience members, known as 'groundlings', stood was not covered.

Public theatres did not have sets or use many **props** but the company spent a lot of money on costumes. There were musicians on stage and music was an integral part of many of Shakespeare's plays.

The actors were all male, the female parts being played by boys or young men. The company performed plays 'in repertory', presenting a different play each day. Members of the company specialised in different roles; Richard Burbage, for example, played tragic heroes and Will Kempe played clowns or **fools**.

How is this reflected in the play?

Because of the lack of scenery, when necessary, Shakespeare establishes very quickly where and when each scene is set, for example, when Lorenzo opens Act 5 with 'The moon shines bright'.

When Gratiano says, 'This is the penthouse under which Lorenzo/Desired us to make stand' (IIvi), he is standing under the balcony or gallery. In the following scene when Portia tells a servant to 'draw aside the curtains', she is referring to curtains across the recess at the back of the stage.

In *The Merchant of Venice* all three women disguise themselves as men or boys. This happens in several of Shakespeare's comedies. While this is partly to enable the characters to do things women would not be expected to do, it is also something of a joke, playing on the audience's knowledge that the actors were really male.

Launcelot Gobbo is described as a 'clown' and it is likely that the part was especially written for Will Kempe to show off his comedy skills. Richard Burbage probably played Shylock, suggesting that Shakespeare may have seen the character almost as a tragic hero.

In what ways is *The Merchant of Venice* a comedy?

The Merchant of Venice includes clowning from the Gobbos and witty banter between other characters but, in this context, a comedy is not a play whose main purpose is to make people laugh. It is a play that ends happily or in which order is restored without the major characters dying.

Like other Shakespearean comedies, *The Merchant of Venice* centres on love, which is put at risk by misunderstandings but ends in marriage.

Shakespeare's comedies often contain fairy-tale-like plots, such as the choosing of the caskets. They also involve events that are absurdly unrealistic but are accepted by the audience, such as Portia pretending to be a male lawyer.

Summary

- When Shakespeare wrote the play, he was one of England's leading writers.
- It was first performed in a public theatre, the design of which is used in the play.
- Female roles were played by boys or young men.

Questions

QUICK TEST
1. What was the name of Shakespeare's company of actors?
2. Name two of Shakespeare's leading actors.
3. For which scene does Shakespeare use the curtained area at the back of the stage?

EXAM PRACTICE
Write a paragraph exploring how Shakespeare uses music in *The Merchant of Venice*.

Gender Roles

You must be able to: understand the importance of gender roles in the Elizabethan era and how this is reflected in the play.

What is meant by gender roles?

At different times and in different places, men and women are expected to play different parts in society.

Elizabethan men generally had more power than women. However, it is important to remember that political and social power was limited to a very small number of people and the most powerful of these was a woman, Queen Elizabeth I.

Upper-class women might expect to have their husbands chosen for them by their fathers or (if their fathers were dead) their brothers. Married women did not own property and were expected to obey their husbands. In return, men were expected to provide for their wives.

Widows and single women could own property and there were quite a few examples of powerful and influential widows. Queen Elizabeth did not marry: this may have been because she did not want to share power with a husband, as her sister Mary I had.

Girls did not go school and could not attend university or enter professions such as the law. Upper-class women, like the Queen, were often very well educated privately.

The main role of middle- and working-class women was that of wife and mother but some women did work in areas such as agriculture, domestic service and trade.

How are gender roles presented in the play?

Portia accepts that, even after his death, her father should be obeyed and should influence her choice of husband. She hands over all her property and wealth to Bassanio.

Jessica, however, disobeys her father and marries against his wishes. Her disobedience is made worse for her father by the fact that she is 'marrying out' of her religion and culture, but audiences would probably sympathise with her. Nerissa appears to be free to choose her own husband, perhaps because she is from a lower social class than Portia.

Portia is clearly well-educated and confident but she and Nerissa have to disguise themselves as men in order to appear in court. Their disguise allows them to behave more freely, travelling unaccompanied and talking openly with men.

Shakespeare often has his heroines disguise themselves as men so that they can act independently, influencing the plot and demonstrating their intellectual equality with men.

Older male characters are shown playing active roles in society, whether trading like Antonio and Shylock, ruling like the Duke or teaching law like the unseen Bellario.

The young men seem to spend their time enjoying themselves and falling in love, although Bassanio has been a soldier. Portia makes fun of young men as 'bragging Jacks' when she describes how she intends to imitate a man.

Summary

- Upper-class men often chose their daughters' husbands.
- Married women could not own property and were expected to obey their husbands.
- Widows and single women had more independence than married women.
- Portia's disguise gives her freedom and independence.

Questions

QUICK TEST

1. Name two things no women could do.
2. What sort of women could own property?
3. What would make Jessica's disobedience worse for Shylock?

EXAM PRACTICE

Portia: But now, I was the lord
            Of this fair mansion, master of my servants,
            Queen o'er myself; and even now, but now,
            This house, these servants, and this same myself,
            Are yours, my lord's. (IIIii)

Relating your ideas to the historical context of Elizabethan gender roles, write a paragraph explaining how Shakespeare presents Portia's marriage to Bassanio.

You must be able to: understand the significance of classical mythology in *The Merchant of Venice*.

What is classical mythology?

The term 'classical mythology' refers to stories about gods and heroes that originated in ancient Greece and Rome. There are many references to classical mythology in the play.

Which classical heroes are presented in the play?

Hercules and Jason are both mentioned. Many members of the Elizabethan audience would have been familiar with their stories.

Hercules (also called Alcides) is known for his enormous strength and the twelve 'Labours of Hercules', a series of seemingly impossible tasks that he was set. In a separate story, Hercules rescues Hesione, the daughter of the King of Troy. She has been tied to a rock, waiting to be eaten by a sea monster, as a sacrifice to the sea god. The king promises Hercules horses as a reward but does not keep his bargain.

Jason is best known for his quest for the Golden Fleece (the coat of a gold-haired winged ram), another supposedly impossible task. The fleece is guarded by a dragon in the kingdom of Aetes. Jason is helped to overcome the dragon by Medea, the king's daughter.

What is the significance of Hercules and Jason in the play?

Both heroes are known for their cleverness as well as their strength. The Prince of Morocco identifies with Hercules but the story he mentions involves Hercules losing a game of dice, which foreshadows the Prince's losing in Portia's 'lottery'.

Portia refers to the story of Hercules and Hesione as Bassanio is choosing. This shows that she thinks of him as a hero. Like Hesione, she has been put in danger by her father. She shows awareness of the fact that Hercules was not motivated by love but by the reward he was promised, saying that Bassanio has 'more love' than Hercules.

Bassanio refers to the story of the Golden Fleece when he is telling Antonio about Portia. Gratiano mentions it again after Bassanio has chosen correctly. Portia is identified with the fleece rather than with Medea. Unlike Medea, she does not betray her father or help Bassanio with his choice.

Which classical lovers are mentioned?

At the beginning of Act 5, Jessica and Lorenzo compare their own story to several classical love stories, including that of Jason and Medea.

Thisbe arranges to meet Pyramus to run away. However, she is frightened by a lion, which tears her scarf. When Pyramus sees this, thinking the lion has killed Thisbe, he kills himself. She then returns and kills herself.

Dido, the Queen of Carthage, falls in love with Aeneas but he abandons her and goes on to found Rome. She kills herself.

Troilus and Cressida is a medieval story set during the **Trojan war**. The Trojan Prince Troilus's lover, Cressida, is captured by the Greeks. He goes to find her but catches her with another man.

What is their significance in the play?

The beginning of Act 5 sets a gentle and romantic mood, with Jessica and Lorenzo apparently happy as they reflect on their own love story. However, the classical stories they mention give the conversation an **ambiguous** tone, preparing the audience for the **denouement** of the 'ring' plot.

None of the stories end well, with two of the heroines killing themselves. Medea betrays her father to run away with her lover, reflecting Lorenzo and Jessica's story. Troilus is betrayed by Cressida and Dido is betrayed by Aeneas.

Summary

- There are references to classical stories throughout the play.
- Hercules and Jason both succeed in apparently impossible tasks.
- Jessica and Lorenzo compare themselves to lovers whose stories do not end well.

Questions

QUICK TEST
1. Who sacrifices Hesione to the sea god?
2. To which object does Bassanio implicitly compare Portia?
3. Who betrays her father to help Jason?

EXAM PRACTICE

Portia: Now he goes,
         With no less presence, but with much more love,
         Than young Alcides, when he did redeem
         The virgin tribute paid by howling Troy
         To the sea-monster. (IIIii)

Write a paragraph explaining how Shakespeare uses classical mythology to explore the relationship between Portia and Bassanio.

The Bible

What is the Bible?

The Bible is the holy book of both the Jewish and Christian faiths.

The Old Testament is an account of God's creation of the world and the history of the Jewish people, read and revered by both Jews and Christians. It includes the story of God giving the Ten Commandments to Moses. These commandments form the basis of both Jewish and Christian morality.

The New Testament describes the life and teachings of Jesus Christ. For Christians, it is more important than the Old Testament. Jews do not accept it.

Even though most people in Elizabethan England could not read, they would know the Bible well because extracts were read (as they are today) in church. For those who could read, the Bible and prayer books were usually their main reading matter.

How do characters use the Old Testament?

Shylock often refers to the Bible, helping to establish his Jewish identity. He uses a story about Jacob tricking his father-in-law, who had broken an agreement about who would own certain sheep, to justify lending money for interest. Antonio disagrees about the meaning of the story. This illustrates the old idea that the Bible can be used to support any idea or opinion.

Shylock compares Portia to the young judge Daniel in the Bible, a model of youthful wisdom, only for his words to be turned against him by Gratiano.

Shylock refers to Launcelot Gobbo as 'Hagar's offspring'. Hagar was a slave of Abraham. She gave birth to his son, Ishmael. The Jewish people are descended from Isaac, the son of Abraham and his wife Sarah. As Ishmael was an outcast born to a slave, this is an insult that **implies** that not just Launcelot but all Christians are inferior.

Talking to Jessica, Launcelot refers to 'the sins of the father', the idea that guilt can be passed from generation to generation. This comes from the Book of Exodus in the Old Testament but is contradicted in other places in the Old Testament. It is also rejected in the New Testament. He may be showing genuine concern for Jessica (he often refers to her father as a 'devil') or just using her Jewish background as the starting point of an elaborate joke.

How do characters use the New Testament?

Shylock shows a surprising knowledge of the New Testament when he compares Bassanio to the **prodigal son** in the **parable**. Although meant as an insult, it is an appropriate comparison as the son in the story wastes his father's money but is forgiven and welcomed back by his father. The parable is an illustration of God's forgiving nature.

Shylock also shows contempt for Christianity by calling Christ the 'Nazarite prophet'. He compares Antonio to a 'fawning **publican**', which Christians would recognise as an insult because of references in the New Testament to 'publicans and sinners'.

Portia refers to the Lord's Prayer, the prayer taught to his followers by Christ, to back up her argument that mercy comes from God and will be given to those who show forgiveness to others.

Summary

- Both Jews and Christians revere the Bible as a holy book.
- The characters show that the Bible can be interpreted in different ways.
- Shylock uses the Bible to insult Christians.
- Portia refers to the New Testament when talking about mercy.

Questions

QUICK TEST
1. Which Bible story do Shylock and Antonio disagree about?
2. Who was Hagar?
3. To which parable from the New Testament does Shylock refer?

EXAM PRACTICE
Antonio: 'The devil can cite scripture for his purpose,' (Iiii)

Relating your ideas to the historical context, write a paragraph explaining how Shakespeare uses the Bible to present one or more of the characters in the play.

You must be able to: analyse how Shylock is presented in the play.

Who is Shylock?

Shylock is a Jew who makes a living by lending money to merchants.

What is his function in the play?

Shylock is not the title character and does not appear in many scenes but his actions drive the plot and his presence often dominates productions of the play.

What is his motivation?

Shylock refers to his deal with Antonio as a 'merry bond'. He insists on taking the flesh rather than accepting the money he is owed because, he says, he hates Antonio and he has sworn an oath that he will have it.

In Act 1 scene 3, Shylock says he hates Antonio because he (Antonio) lends money without interest, ruining Shylock's business. Antonio and Shylock argue about **usury**.

Shylock also says that he has been taunted, kicked and spat on by Antonio in the past. Shylock's hatred is a reaction to anti-Semitism. Although Shylock has a general dislike of Christians, his feelings about Antonio are stronger and are clearly related to Antonio's particular behaviour towards him.

Shylock's determination to pursue his bond is increased when he hears about his daughter Jessica's behaviour after eloping with Lorenzo. He blames Antonio and Bassanio's friends for helping her to elope.

Although he displays a love of wealth both when Jessica steals his money and when the court takes away his property, this is not his **motivation** in taking Antonio to court, as he initially turns down a considerable amount of money when Bassanio offers it.

Villain or victim?

Modern productions and audiences tend to view Shylock as a victim of anti-Semitism. In the past, he has sometimes been portrayed as a villain, although many actors throughout the play's history have portrayed him sympathetically.

The text, especially Shylock's speech in Act 3 where he explains why he should have revenge, does not support the idea that Shakespeare intended him to be seen purely as a villain. However, his refusal to show mercy and his enjoyment at the prospect of cutting out Antonio's flesh show a vengeful nature and cause his downfall.

He is certainly a victim of anti-Semitism but to what degree audiences see him as a victim depends on their reaction to his treatment by the court. Many modern audience members consider his conversion to Christianity as the ultimate (and unnecessary) humiliation. However, other audiences (including Elizabethan ones) would have seen this as a good outcome for Shylock and that he had been treated reasonably by the court.

Key Quotations to Learn

Shylock: 'Hath not a Jew eyes?' (IIIi)

Shylock: 'Thou call'dst me a dog before thou hadst a cause; / But since I am a dog, beware my fangs:' (IIIiii)

Shylock: 'An oath, an oath! I have an oath in heaven; / Shall I lay perjury upon my soul?' (IVi)

Summary

- Shylock's actions drive the plot of *The Merchant of Venice*.
- He is motivated by hatred of Antonio, caused by Antonio's treatment of him in the past.
- Audiences are usually sympathetic to Shylock.
- Whether he is a villain or victim – or both – depends on the audience's perception.

Sample Analysis

In Act 3 scene 3, Shylock's anger and determination are shown by his repetition of 'I'll have my bond!'. He mentions the bond three times in both his second and third speeches, emphasising its importance and suggesting he has become obsessed with it. The **caesuras** that break up his lines as he talks of the bond reflect his anger. He refers to Antonio's previous insults, showing that his motivation comes from these as much as from his 'oath'. When he says, 'since I am a dog, beware my fangs' he inverts the **metaphor** 'dog' that Antonio has used to **imply** that Jews are less than human, developing it to threaten Antonio.

Questions

QUICK TEST
1. Who is Shylock's daughter?
2. What has Antonio done to Shylock in the past?
3. What suggests that Shylock wants revenge?

EXAM PRACTICE
Using at least one of the 'Key Quotations to Learn', write a paragraph explaining how Shakespeare presents Shylock's reaction to his treatment by Christians.

Portia

You must be able to: analyse how Portia is presented in the play.

Who is Portia?

Portia is a young heiress. She is named after a Roman woman who was famous as a virtuous and honourable wife.

What is her function in the play?

Portia is the prize for the man who picks the right casket. Bassanio's desire to win her causes Antonio to pledge his bond to Shylock. In Act 4, Portia takes control of the plot.

What is she like?

Portia moves from being the passive object of her suitors' desires to being the active character who untangles the plot and brings about a happy ending.

She is obedient to her dead father but she does not accept his plan without question. Nerissa reminds her that he was 'holy' and 'virtuous' and advises her to have confidence in his plan.

She is perceptive and witty, commenting on the shortcomings of her suitors.

She shows she loves Bassanio by trying to delay his choice but she remains true to her oath by not helping him to choose the correct casket.

Her reaction after his choice also shows that love and duty are intertwined for her. She makes him her 'lord' willingly.

Why does she disguise herself as a man?

She has to disguise herself as a man to appear in the court. Bringing her into the court allows Shakespeare to show a female character taking control of the action.

Her disguise provides **dramatic irony** as Bassanio talks to her about his wife, not realising who she is.

It also enables her to 'test' Bassanio by asking for the ring. This test suggests that their love may not be as strong as it seemed at first.

How is she presented in the trial scene?

The Duke allows her to take over the court and act as a judge.

Bellario praises her 'learning' and she shows herself to be confident, clever and eloquent.

She is determined that the law is applied, saying that the laws of Venice cannot be changed. However, she asks Shylock, the Duke and Antonio to show mercy, suggesting that she is not interested in revenge.

She is motivated by her love for Bassanio.

What is Portia like at the end of the play?

Portia may have given her property to Bassanio, but she remains in control as she welcomes other characters to Belmont and ties up loose ends in Act 5.

She accepts Bassanio's explanation of why he gave away the ring but the audience might doubt the strength of his love and wonder whether her experiences have altered her.

Key Quotations to Learn

Portia: 'Away then, I am locked in one of them. / If you do love me, you will find me out.' (IIIii)

Portia: 'O love, be moderate, allay they ecstasy,' (IIIii)

Shylock: 'A Daniel come to judgement! Yea, a Daniel! / O wise young judge, how I do honour thee!' (IVi)

Summary

- Portia is a prize for the man who chooses wisely.
- Although she has doubts about her father's plan, she obeys and is rewarded with love.
- She dominates the court scene and brings about the play's ending.

Sample Analysis

In her attitude to her father's plan, Portia reveals the tension between her sense of duty and her feelings. She acknowledges that 'the brain may devise laws for the blood' but uses **imagery** to illustrate the power of 'blood', meaning passion or emotion. She **personifies** 'madness' (giving in to passion) as a 'youth', which like a hare leaps over 'good counsel' or wisdom, which is personified as a 'cripple'. This reflects the opposition between her natural desire, as a young woman, to choose her own husband, and the 'will' of her father, which she must obey.

Questions

QUICK TEST
1. Why does Nerissa think Portia should accept her father's lottery?
2. Who has sent 'Balthasar' to Venice?
3. Who does Portia think should show mercy?

EXAM PRACTICE
Using at least one of the 'Key Quotations to Learn', write a paragraph explaining how Shakespeare presents Portia in Act 4 scene 1.

Antonio

You must be able to: analyse how Antonio is presented in the play.

Who is Antonio?

Antonio is the 'Merchant' after whom the play in named.

What is his function in the play?

The plot centres on Antonio's actions, when he agrees to give a pound of flesh as his bond to Shylock and is then taken to court when he cannot pay his debt. Despite this, Antonio is not usually thought of as the play's **protagonist**.

What is Antonio like?

Antonio opens the play by saying he is sad but does not know why. Elizabethan plays often featured characters who were '**melancholy**' and a bit detached from the world.

He is generous towards Bassanio and has been generous to others. Solanio calls him 'good' and 'honest'. Lorenzo praises him to Portia.

Shylock sees another side of Antonio.

What are Antonio's feelings for Bassanio?

Bassanio is Antonio's 'kinsman', meaning they are related. Antonio could be seen as a father figure to Bassanio, an idea supported by him offering his 'flesh' as a bond.

Some audience members might think Antonio's attachment to Bassanio is romantic, as he speaks of his 'love' and calls him 'sweet Bassanio'. However, this could just indicate a strong friendship or attachment between family members.

Antonio has great influence over Bassanio. Bassanio immediately travels to Venice to help him and is persuaded by him to give his ring to 'Balthasar'.

Antonio encourages Bassanio to woo Portia and at the end says he will be 'surety' for his faithfulness.

What are Antonio's feelings towards Shylock?

Antonio claims that Shylock resents him for lending money interest-free, so damaging Shylock's business.

Despite his stand against usury, Antonio does borrow from Shylock. This could show **hypocrisy** and/or the strength of his feelings for Bassanio.

Shylock has other reasons for hating Antonio, as he has often insulted him and even spat on him because he is a Jew. Shylock's account of Antonio's behaviour may create sympathy for him and **antipathy** towards Antonio.

How is Antonio presented in court?

At the start of Act 4, Antonio is patient, reasonable and accepting of his fate. He acts in a dignified way as he prepares to have his flesh cut out.

At the end of the scene, he shows some mercy to Shylock, who has shown none to him, by not taking his property from him.

Key Quotations to Learn

Antonio: 'In sooth I know not why I am so sad.' (Ii)

Shylock: 'You call me misbeliever, cut-throat dog, / And spit upon my Jewish gaberdine,' (Iiii)

Solanio: '… the good Antonio, the honest Antonio –' (IIIi)

Summary

- Antonio puts his life at risk for Bassanio by making a bond with Shylock.
- Shylock hates Antonio because of the way he has treated Shylock in the past.
- Other characters think Antonio is good and honourable.

Sample Analysis

Antonio's love for Bassanio appears at first to be generous and selfless. He breaks 'a custom' of not paying interest to 'supply the ripe wants of my friend' when he deals with his 'enemy' Shylock. This act ultimately puts his life at risk. It also makes Bassanio indebted to him and, though he does not ask for the money, he twice calls in the debt emotionally. First, he summons Bassanio from Belmont on his wedding day, asking to see him before he dies. Later, he persuades him to give away the ring, asking that 'my love withal, /Be valued 'gainst your wife's commandment'. When, having reminded Portia that he 'did lend my body for his wealth', he pledges his 'soul upon the forfeit' that Bassanio will be faithful, the audience might wonder who it is who has most power over Bassanio – Portia or Antonio?

Questions

QUICK TEST
1. What is Antonio's mood when the play opens?
2. What does he persuade Bassanio to do after the trial scene?
3. What is his profession?

EXAM PRACTICE
Using at least one of the 'Key Quotations to Learn', write a paragraph explaining how Shakespeare presents Antonio's relationship with Shylock.

You must be able to: analyse how Bassanio is presented in the play.

Who is Bassanio?

Bassanio is a kinsman of Antonio. He has lost all the wealth that he inherited from his father.

What is his function in the play?

His request to Antonio to lend him some money causes Antonio to make his ill-fated deal with Shylock. He brings together the two worlds of Venice and Belmont.

What is Bassanio's character?

Bassanio is described as a scholar and soldier and he is open about having wasted the money he inherited. His lack of concern for money contrasts with Shylock and, to some extent, with Antonio.

His extravagance might be the result of being open and generous but it creates problems not just for him but for his friend.

He is at the centre of a group of young men who enjoy life, although he is more thoughtful than Gratiano and less daring than Lorenzo.

How are his feelings for Portia presented?

At first, he presents his interest in Portia as an adventure and a way of getting out of debt. However, he goes on to mention her beauty and virtue, and says that he has had 'fair speechless messages' from her eyes.

At Belmont, his language is poetic and romantic, and their love seems to be strong and mutual. His long speech before choosing the casket shows thoughtfulness and wisdom, justifying his reputation as a 'scholar'.

His choice of the lead casket shows him to be more genuine and deserving than either Morocco or Arragon.

What do his actions after his marriage show?

His reaction to Antonio's news shows generosity, a sense of duty and love for his friend, which impress Portia.

He does his best to help Antonio but he fails to convince Shylock to accept the money. It is interesting that where he fails, his wife succeeds. This suggests that, even with the money he lacked before, he is well-meaning but ineffectual and that the protagonist of this play is the woman, not the man.

When 'Balthasar' asks for his ring, Bassanio resists at first because of the oath he has made to Portia, but is persuaded by Antonio. This calls into question the strength of his love for Portia and his trustworthiness.

When challenged by Portia he admits the truth, although not until Gratiano has already done so, swearing another oath to be faithful. The audience might wonder whether he is capable of keeping this oath.

Key Quotations to Learn

Nerissa: 'He, of all the men that ever my foolish eyes looked upon, was the best deserving a fair lady.' (Iii)

Bassanio: 'Let me choose, / For as I am, I live upon the rack.' (IIIii)

Bassanio: 'But when this ring / Parts from this finger, then parts life from hence;' (IIIii)

Summary

- Bassanio is a soldier and scholar who has spent his inheritance.
- He shows his worth by choosing the right casket.
- He breaks his oath to Portia when he gives away the ring.

Sample Analysis

Before making his choice, Bassanio speaks **eloquently** about a world 'deceived with ornament' and supports his argument with examples from different aspects of life. His rejection of gold and silver for 'meagre lead' implies that he is motivated by love, not greed and is, therefore, genuine and the worthy winner of Portia's hand. Yet, he has spoken of marriage to Portia as a way 'to get clear of all the debts', and subsequent events cast doubt on his honesty. Almost immediately, he is forced to admit that he is not just poor but in debt. He goes on to break his oath when he gives away the ring and, when challenged about it, considers lying before Gratiano leaves him with no choice but to be truthful.

Questions

QUICK TEST
1. Who gives Bassanio the money to help him woo Portia?
2. What does his choice of casket show?
3. How does he try to persuade Shylock not to take his pound of flesh?

EXAM PRACTICE
Using at least one of the 'Key Quotations to Learn', write a paragraph explaining how Shakespeare presents Bassanio as an adventurer.

Gratiano and Nerissa

You must be able to: analyse how Gratiano and Nerissa are presented in the play.

Who is Gratiano?

Gratiano is a friend of Bassanio.

What is his function in the play?

He acts as companion to Bassanio, going with him to Belmont. His relationship with Nerissa mirrors Bassanio's relationship with Portia.

What is his character?

He is lively and excitable. He says he wants to 'play the fool and enjoy life'. He throws himself into Lorenzo's plot to elope with Jessica. Bassanio thinks he talks too much and says he will have to calm down when he goes to Belmont. He is immature compared to Bassanio.

He follows Bassanio around and imitates his actions.

He is impetuous, both in deciding to go to Belmont and in marrying Nerissa. He can be quite crude, making sexual **innuendos** and references. Portia tells him to 'speak not so grossly'.

In the court scene, he enjoys baiting Shylock, shouting comments from the sidelines. This behaviour contrasts with that of the more restrained and serious Bassanio.

Who is Nerissa?

Nerissa is Portia's 'waiting woman', a sort of superior servant, more of a companion than a maid.

What is her function in the play?

She is Portia's **confidante**, supporting her both at Belmont and in Venice. Her questions allow Portia to express her feelings.

What is her character?

She is perceptive and gives good advice to Portia about her father's 'lottery' and about Bassanio.

She is faithful to Portia and follows her without question. She imitates Porta's behaviour by testing Gratiano's faithfulness.

What is their relationship like?

We are not shown how or why they fall in love, just that Gratiano has sworn 'oaths' of love and Nerissa has agreed to marry him only if Bassanio is successful.

Their relationship is a shadow of Bassanio and Portia's, following the same plot but expressed more crudely and comically. Gratiano proposes having a bet on who has the first son and in his final speech he dwells on the coming **consummation** of his marriage.

Key Quotations to Learn

Bassanio: 'Gratiano speaks an infinite deal of nothing, more than any man in all Venice.' (Ii)

Nerissa (to Portia): 'Your father was ever virtuous, and holy men at their deaths have good inspirations;' (Iii)

Bassanio (to Gratiano): 'Thou art too wild, too rude and bold of voice –' (IIiii)

Summary

- Gratiano is lively, spontaneous and sometimes crude.
- Nerissa is a faithful confidante to Portia.
- Their relationship mirrors the relationship of Portia and Bassanio, and they imitate their actions.
- Like Bassanio, Gratiano fails his wife's test and gives away his ring.

Sample Analysis

Gratiano responds to Antonio's assertion that the world is 'a stage where every man must play his part' by claiming that his part is that of a 'fool'. While Antonio's statement implies that he believes in **pre-destination** and that he has been given a 'sad' character that he cannot change, Gratiano's response suggests that he believes he can choose his personality. He wants to be ruled by his 'blood', or passion, something also mentioned by Portia and Bassanio. When he speaks of his 'grandsire cut in alabaster' he is referring to the cold stone from which tombs were often made. For him, Antonio might as well be dead as he does not embrace life in the way Gratiano does.

Questions

QUICK TEST
1. What is Nerissa's position in Portia's household?
2. Who says Gratiano talks too much?
3. Who tells Gratiano off for the way he talks?
4. What is Nerissa's condition for marrying Gratiano?

EXAM PRACTICE
Using at least one of the 'Key Quotations to Learn', write a paragraph explaining how Shakespeare presents the character of Gratiano.

Lorenzo and Jessica

You must be able to: analyse how Lorenzo and Jessica are presented in the play.

Who is Lorenzo?

Lorenzo is a friend of Bassanio and Gratiano.

What is his function in the play?

By eloping with Jessica, he shows another aspect of love and helps to motivate Shylock by increasing his resentment of Christians.

What is his character?

Lorenzo is defined by his love for Jessica. He is first seen preparing to elope with her and almost everything he says is about her or his love for her.

His seriousness contrasts with Gratiano's frivolity. He sees good in others, praising both Portia and Antonio's virtues.

He is more light-hearted when talking to Jessica at Belmont, although their joking references to classical lovers have an undercurrent of sadness.

Who is Jessica and what is her function in the play?

Jessica is Shylock's daughter.

Her relationship with Shylock shows another side of him and her elopement with Lorenzo increases his desire for revenge.

What is her character?

She is seen mostly through the eyes of Lorenzo, who thinks she is perfect: 'wise, fair and true'.

In the only scene that Jessica and Shylock have together, he tells her to lock herself in and not look at the masque. She tells Launcelot Gobbo that 'our house is hell', suggesting her elopement is motivated by a desire to escape from Shylock as well as by love.

Her escape from Venice shows independence and determination as well as her love for Lorenzo. Her journey from Venice to Belmont disguised as a boy anticipates Portia's journey from Belmont to Venice.

Shylock's reaction to her escape shows a sense of betrayal that is mixed comically with his anger at her stealing his money. His desire to see her 'dead at my foot' reflects the idea that by marrying a Christian she would be 'dead' to her family. However, when he hears from Tubal that she has exchanged the ring his wife gave him for a monkey, audiences might sympathise more with him than with her.

What is Jessica and Lorenzo's relationship like?

They are in love from the start of the play and their relationship does not change.

It is similar to Bassanio and Portia's relationship in that by marrying Jessica, Lorenzo becomes rich, although in Lorenzo's case, this is unexpected and is not part of his motivation.

In contrast to Portia, Jessica disobeys her father to find love.

Despite their conversation at Belmont being about betrayal and unfaithful lovers, Jessica does not 'test' Lorenzo the way Portia and Nerissa test their future husbands.

Key Quotations to Learn

Jessica: 'Alack, what heinous sin is it in me / To be ashamed to be my father's child!' (IIiii)

Lorenzo: 'For she is wise, if I can judge of her, / And fair she is, if that mine eyes be true, / And true she is, as she has proved herself;' (IIvi)

Solanio (quoting Shylock): 'My daughter! O my ducats! O my daughter!' (IIviii)

Summary

- Lorenzo and Jessica are in love from the start and do not change.
- Jessica, unlike Portia, disobeys her father.
- Lorenzo gets rich by marrying Jessica but he has not married her for money.

Sample Analysis

In contrast with Portia, Jessica defies her father when she marries Lorenzo. He tries to keep her physically locked away from 'Christian fools', unaware that she has already made plans for escape. Her attitude to her father differs from that of Portia, who accepts that her father is 'wise' and has her interests at heart. Jessica describes her home as 'hell' and says she is 'ashamed to be' Shylock's child. Her statement that she is not a daughter 'to his manners' could imply a rejection of his religion as well as of his behaviour, an impression strengthened by her determination to convert to Christianity. Nevertheless, she acknowledges that such feelings towards her father are a 'heinous sin', reflecting the expectation that daughters should obey their fathers.

Questions

QUICK TEST
1. Who is praised by Lorenzo?
2. What does Jessica take in exchange for a ring?
3. To what does she compare Shylock's house?

EXAM PRACTICE
Using at least one of the 'Key Quotations to Learn', write a paragraph explaining how Shakespeare presents the relationship between Lorenzo and Jessica.

The Prince of Morocco, the Prince of Arragon and the Duke

You must be able to: analyse how the two princes and the Duke are presented in the play.

Who is the Prince of Morocco?

He is a powerful man from Morocco in North Africa. The fact that he is a prince shows the sort of man Portia might expect to marry – unlike the poor 'gentleman' Bassanio.

He mentions his dark 'complexion'. When she says it makes no difference to her, she demonstrates her willingness to obey her father and marry whoever chooses correctly.

He boasts of his past military exploits and compares himself to Hercules.

He chooses the golden casket, thinking that Portia is 'what all men desire' but opens it to reveal a symbol of death.

Who is the Prince of Arragon?

Like Morocco, he is rich and powerful. Arragon is part of Spain; Shakespeare may have chosen the name as a pun on 'arrogant'.

He is more cautious than Morocco and rejects gold because he does not want to be like 'all men'. He chooses silver because he thinks he should get what he deserves. He opens the casket to reveal the image of a fool.

What is the function of the princes?

Their presence shows how wealthy and beautiful Portia is, and how far around the world her reputation and the story of the caskets have spread.

Their choices create some tension as the audience, with Portia, waits to see what choice they make and what is inside each casket.

Morocco and Arragon prepare the audience for Bassanio's choice. Compared to them he is the 'underdog' and is likely to have the audience's sympathy as he takes his gamble, both because he is poor and because he and Portia are in love.

Their incorrect choices show their failure to see beyond the surface and their unwillingness to 'hazard' or risk everything they have for love.

Who is the Duke and what does he do?

The Duke is Shakespeare's version of the Doge, Venice's elected ruler.

He only appears in Act 4, where he represents the state of Venice and its system of justice.

He shows sympathy to Antonio and urges Shylock to be merciful but then steps back from the dispute, allowing Portia to interpret the law and so decide what should happen.

Through him, the law of Venice is shown to be neutral and unalterable. He can, however, give mercy, which he does by not condemning Shylock to death and proposing that he pays a fine instead of giving half his property to the state.

Portia: 'O these deliberate fools! When they do choose, / They have the wisdom by their wit to lose.' (IIix)

Duke: 'How shalt thou hope for mercy, rendering none?' (IVi)

Duke: 'That thou shalt see the difference of our spirit, / I pardon thee thy life before thou ask it;' (IVi)

Summary

- Morocco and Arragon are powerful and rich but choose the wrong caskets.
- The Duke represents the power and justice of Venice.
- The Duke shows mercy to Shylock.

Sample Analysis

The first words that the Duke addresses to Antonio are 'I am sorry for thee'. He might be speaking for the audience, almost directing its sympathy, as well as for Venice. This implies that he biased. The way he speaks about Shylock confirms this impression, as he calls him 'an inhuman wretch' who is 'uncapable of pity'. Although the Duke does not express an opinion about Jews in general, this characterisation reflects anti-Semitic **stereotypes**. He goes on to plead for a 'gentle answer' from Shylock but, ultimately, he is bound by the law and he cannot interfere with the bargain they have made.

Questions

QUICK TEST
1. What does the Duke ask Shylock to do?
2. To which classical hero does the Prince of Morocco compare himself?
3. Why does the Prince of Arragon choose silver?

EXAM PRACTICE
Using at least one of the 'Key Quotations to Learn', write a paragraph explaining the role and significance of the Duke.

You must be able to: analyse how these characters are presented in the play.

Who are the Gobbos?

Launcelot Gobbo is Shylock's servant, who leaves him to work for Bassanio.

Old Gobbo is his father, who has come to Venice looking for his son.

What is their function in the play?

Launcelot is a clown or fool and his main function in the play is to provide comedy in his interactions with other characters.

He occasionally helps the plot along, for example, by taking Jessica's letter to Lorenzo.

Old Gobbo only appears in one scene. He provides one half of a comic double-act with his son. 'Gobbo' is Italian for **hunchback**: this and Old Gobbo's poor eyesight indicate the kind of broad visual comedy their meeting might provide.

Launcelot provides humour through his use of puns, playing on words and 'chop logic'. This means putting forward complicated arguments that seem logical but make little or no sense.

Launcelot 'tests' his half-blind father by pretending that he is someone else and that Launcelot is dead, so that he can hear himself praised. This prefigures Portia's testing of Bassanio's love.

Old Gobbo is one of several fathers who appear or are mentioned in the play. His relationship with Launcelot can be compared with Jessica's relationship with Shylock. Gobbo's literal blindness reflects Shylock's blindness to what Jessica is doing. Like Jessica, Launcelot deceives his father (although for him it is a joke). The Gobbos are reunited shortly before Shylock and Jessica are parted.

Who are Solanio and Salerio?

Solanio and Salerio are friends of Antonio and Bassanio. They usually appear together and are not given distinct characters.

What is their function in the play?

They provide a kind of **chorus** in the play, talking about what has happened and speculating on what might happen next.

They represent the citizens of Venice. Their attitudes to Shylock and Antonio, and their reactions to events, reflect those of the typical citizen.

Sometimes they have a role in advancing the plot, for example, when they help Lorenzo and when Salerio brings the news about Antonio to Belmont.

Key Quotations to Learn

Gobbo: 'The boy was the very staff of my age, my very prop.' (IIii)

Salerio (of Antonio): 'A kinder gentleman treads not the earth.' (IIviii)

Lorenzo: 'How every fool can play upon the word!' (IIIv)

Summary

- Solanio and Salerio comment on the action and represent the citizens of Venice.
- Launcelot and Old Gobbo show broad visual and verbal comedy.
- They are an example of a father/child relationship.

Sample Analysis

At the beginning of Act 3, Solanio and Salerio set the scene for the audience when Solanio asks his friend for 'news on the Rialto', reminding us that we are in Venice, which is at the centre of international trade. In their last scene, Solanio warns that Antonio might 'pay' for Shylock's anger at Jessica and Salerio gives news of a ship being wrecked in the English Channel, giving hints of trouble to come. They express concern for 'the honest Antonio', anticipating the coming conflict between Shylock and Antonio, and making their sympathies, and those of the citizens of Venice, clear. In this way, they fulfil the role of a Greek chorus: giving news, speculating on what is to come and representing the views of the citizens and perhaps the audience.

Questions

QUICK TEST
1. Which characters act as a 'chorus' in the play?
2. For which two characters does Launcelot Gobbo work?
3. What false news does Launcelot give his father?

EXAM PRACTICE
Using at least one of the 'Key Quotations to Learn', write a paragraph explaining the role and significance of Launcelot Gobbo.

Anti-Semitism

You must be able to: analyse how Shakespeare presents the theme of anti-Semitism.

What is anti-Semitism?

Anti-Semitism means prejudice against or hatred of Jewish people.

How is anti-Semitism presented in the play?

Shylock accuses Antonio of insulting him, spitting on him and kicking him because he is a Jew. Far from denying this, Antonio says he would do it again.

Solanio calls Shylock 'the dog Jew', echoing Antonio's language and implying that he is less than human. He also refers to Shylock as the devil 'in the likeness of a Jew'.

In the court, Gratiano ridicules Shylock's praise of Portia. While he does not openly make fun of Shylock's religion, he draws attention to it by addressing him as 'Jew' and 'infidel'.

These characters may have valid personal reasons for disliking Shylock but the audience can **infer** from the constant references to his Judaism that part of their hatred of him is because he is a Jew.

Is society in general shown as anti-Semitic?

Salerio and Solanio represent the **norm** in Venetian society, which suggests that most Christians in Venice are anti-Semitic.

Both the Duke and Portia address Shylock as 'Jew', implying that he does not deserve to be addressed respectfully. Apart from this, their language does not suggest hatred or prejudice. Bassanio calls Shylock a 'devil' but does not refer to his race or religion.

The state of Venice might be seen as anti-Semitic because of the law that punishes 'aliens' with death for threatening the lives of Venetian citizens. Shylock is considered an alien, or foreigner. However, an 'alien' is not specifically a Jew: the same law would apply to anyone from outside Venice.

Is the play itself anti-Semitic?

Some people think it is anti-Semitic because it is about a Jewish man who conforms to some stereotypes of Jewish people: he loves money and he is vengeful and unforgiving. Also, his punishment and humiliation are shown as good things – part of a happy ending.

Others argue that in Shylock, Shakespeare has created a complex character with whom audiences sympathise. He has given him speeches in which he speaks passionately about the abuse he has suffered through anti-Semitism, as well as expressing his own hatred of Christians.

It is important, as with any play, to be aware that different audiences bring with them different attitudes and assumptions, often shaped by the society in which they live.

Key Quotations to Learn

Salerio: 'As the dog Jew did utter in the streets, – / "My daughter! O my ducats! O my daughter!"' (IIviii)

Shylock: 'If you prick us, do we not bleed? If you tickle us, do we not laugh? If you poison us, do we not die?' (IIIi)

Shylock: '... cursed be my tribe / If I forgive him!' (Iiii)

Summary

- Shylock is presented as a victim of anti-Semitism.
- Antonio hates Shylock both for personal reasons and because he is a Jew.
- Anti-Semitism is the norm in the society shown in the play.
- Whether the play itself is anti-Semitic is a matter of opinion.

Sample Analysis

Solanio's account of Shylock's distress after his daughter's elopement focusses on his Jewishness, using **derogatory** language that can leave the audience in little doubt about his anti-Semitism. The **juxtaposition** of the words 'villain' and 'Jew' link Shylock's perceived evil nature to his religion and race. When he calls him 'the dog Jew', using the same animal metaphor as Antonio did earlier, he confirms his prejudice with a suggestion that Jews are less than human. That Solanio should speak like this suggests the whole of Venetian society is anti-Semitic, an impression confirmed by his report of 'all the boys in Venice' taunting Shylock.

Questions

QUICK TEST
1. Which Jewish characters are depicted in the play?
2. Whose attitudes to Jews represent the norm in Venetian society?
3. Who can be punished by death for threatening the lives of Venetians?

EXAM PRACTICE
Using one or more of the 'Key Quotations to Learn', write a paragraph analysing how Shakespeare presents at least one character in the play as anti-Semitic.

You must be able to: analyse how Shakespeare presents ideas about religion in the play.

What ideas about religion does Shakespeare present?

Religion is shown to be part of the fabric of life in Venice, as it was in Elizabethan England. It is assumed that everyone believes in God and in life after death.

In *The Merchant of Venice*, Shakespeare presents two religions in opposition: Judaism and Christianity.

Traditionally, although both religions believe that good acts will be rewarded and evil ones will be punished after death, Judaism places more emphasis on justice while Christianity stresses forgiveness.

How do characters present religious ideas?

Shylock goes to the **synagogue** to swear an oath that he will have his bond. This makes gaining the pound of flesh a religious obligation for him. Elizabethans would see his pursuit of justice and determination to follow the letter of the law, rather than its spirit, as being typically Jewish.

When Portia talks about not deserving salvation but being granted it through God's mercy, she is referring to the Christian idea of the merciful and forgiving God. Shylock's refusal to be merciful might be seen as showing the difference between the two religions. The Duke refers to this when he speaks of 'the difference of our spirit'. However, the concept of God's mercy is an important part of the Jewish faith.

Followers of both religions would think that belonging to their religion was the only way to be saved. Therefore, Shylock is referred to as 'faithless' and 'a devil' and Jessica is called a 'beautiful pagan' by Launcelot Gobbo.

When Launcelot tells Jessica she is damned for being Shylock's daughter, she replies that she has been saved by her husband, who has made her a Christian.

In contrast with Portia's concern with mercy and salvation, Launcelot's version of religion focusses on the devil and damnation, identifying Shylock with the devil. His thinking is muddled and his ideas are more like **superstition** than religious belief. As he is the clown, Shakespeare might be using him to poke fun at some Christians.

Shylock points out some of the shortcomings of Christians in following their religion, for example, in the way they pursue revenge despite Christian teaching about 'turning the other cheek' and their implied hypocrisy in condemning both usury and Judaism but borrowing money from Jews.

Key Quotations to Learn

Shylock: 'If a Jew wrong a Christian, what is his humility? Revenge. If a Christian wrong a Jew, what should his sufferance be by Christian example? Why, revenge!' (IIIi)

Jessica: 'I shall be saved by my husband. He hath made me a Christian.' (IIIv)

Portia: 'Though justice is thy plea, consider this: / That in the course of justice none of us / Shall see salvation:' (IVi)

Summary

- Judaism and Christianity are placed in opposition to each other in the play.
- Shylock takes an oath to pursue his bond.
- The Christians believe that to be 'saved' people must become Christians.
- Shylock exposes differences between Christian beliefs and the practice of Christians.

Sample Analysis

Portia argues that mercy is an 'attribute of God himself', appealing to Shylock's religious belief. Some Elizabethan audience members might have felt that this was pointless as Jews were not interested in mercy or forgiveness, only justice. However, God's mercy is a feature of Jewish religious teaching and it may be that Shakespeare, through Portia, is showing his awareness of this. This idea is supported by the fact that she does not **overtly** refer to Christ or Christianity, suggesting a sensitivity to the beliefs of others not shown elsewhere, although she does refer to 'The Lord's Prayer', which 'doth teach us all to render/the deeds of mercy'.

Questions

QUICK TEST
1. Where does Shylock go to make his oath?
2. How does Jessica think she has been saved?
3. What suggests that Launcelot Gobbo's version of religion is ridiculous?

EXAM PRACTICE
Using one or more of the 'Key Quotations to Learn', write a paragraph analysing how Shakespeare presents Shylock's attitude to Christianity.

Love and Marriage

You must be able to: analyse how Shakespeare presents ideas about love and marriage

How are ideas about love and courtship explored in the play?

Bassanio's courtship of Portia is presented as an adventure. The challenge set by Portia's father makes it like a courtship in a fairy tale.

He proves himself worthy of Portia's love. However, there is also an element of luck, with words such as 'hazard' and 'lottery' used. This could suggest either the randomness of life and love or the idea that Fate determines what happens in life.

Bassanio speaks to Antonio about his possible marriage to Portia as if it is an investment. However, he praises her beauty and virtue.

Portia's love is simpler. She shows her interest in him before he arrives at Belmont. The scene before he chooses the caskets shows how much she feels for him.

In Jessica and Lorenzo's relationship, it is Jessica who may have mixed motives. She is anxious to get away from Shylock. Lorenzo is clearly besotted with her.

Lorenzo is not interested in financial gain. He defies **convention** by marrying a Jew. Jessica also defies society by marrying against her father's wishes, in contrast to Portia's obedience to her father.

Nerissa and Gratiano's love comes out of the blue. Neither of them says why they love each other.

Both Portia and Bassanio mention 'blood' when talking about their feelings, indicating a sexual attraction. The sexual side of marriage is referred to by Gratiano at the end of the play when he refers to consummating his marriage.

The combination of sexual attraction, appreciation of each other's qualities and financial security might make Portia and Bassanio's marriage the ideal relationship.

How are ideas about marriage explored?

Usually in Shakespeare's comedies, the marriages come at the end of the play after various obstacles have been overcome. Here, the couples are married by the end of Act 3 and face a challenge after marriage, although it is significant that their marriages have not been consummated.

Portia and Nerissa give their husbands rings, symbols of love and faithfulness. They emphasise this by making the men swear never to part with their rings.

Bassanio and Gratiano's failure to keep their promises calls into question the strength of their love and the worth of their oaths. Although the wives accept their explanations there is a sense at the end that marriage might not be as easy as falling in love. Some might also feel that, despite their vows to obey their husbands, the wives are now in control.

Key Quotations to Learn

Bassanio: '... sometimes from her eyes / I did receive fair speechless messages:' (Ii)

Portia: 'In terms of choice I am not solely led / By nice direction of a maiden's eyes;' (IIi)

Portia: 'O love, be moderate, allay thy ecstasy,' (IIIii)

Summary

- Bassanio and Lorenzo's courtships follow different, contrasting paths.
- Bassanio and Jessica have mixed motives for getting married.
- Marriage does not represent the end of the story for the three couples.

Sample Analysis

Portia offers herself to Bassanio in a speech that depicts marriage as a willing submission by a woman to her husband. Despite her riches, beauty and wit, she paints herself as a 'an unlessoned girl, unschooled, unpractised'. This **alliterative** triplet gives Bassanio the authority of a teacher over a pupil. She goes to describe him, in another triplet, as 'her lord, her governor, her king'. This reflects the conventional idea that a woman should obey her husband. From being the 'lord' and 'Queen' she has become a servant and a subject. However, it is also an expression of the strength of her love. Bassanio uses similar language to express his feelings for her, comparing her to a 'beloved prince'.

Questions

QUICK TEST

1. How does Lorenzo defy convention?
2. What does Portia's use of the words 'blood' and 'ecstasy' suggest?
3. What is unusual about the marriages in the play compared with other Shakespeare comedies?

EXAM PRACTICE

Using one or more of the 'Key Quotations to Learn', write a paragraph analysing how Shakespeare presents ideas about marriage.

Money and Trade

You must be able to: analyse how Shakespeare presents ideas about money and trade.

Which characters are used to explore ideas about money and trade?

The main characters have different attitudes to money.

Shylock makes money from lending money. He loves money and property. He is described by others as 'rich'.

Antonio makes money from trade. His business is risky. He lends money to others, charging no interest.

Bassanio has wasted his money by living an extravagant life. His marriage to Portia solves his money problems.

Portia has inherited money from her father. On marriage, her property becomes Bassanio's property.

Jessica steals money from her father, which she spends extravagantly. She and Lorenzo will inherit Shylock's property after his death.

How are ideas about trade presented?

Venice depends on trade for its existence. That trade, in turn, depends on money being available. Christians are not allowed to lend money for interest because it is considered a sin. Jews do not share this belief, and so are necessary for Venice's trade.

In this way, Jews and Christians are shown to be interdependent. The Christians could be seen as hypocritical for condemning money-lending but making use of it.

Shylock sees his trade as being no different from a trade like Antonio's. He refers to his profit making, which Christians call usury, as 'thrift'. This implies that it is a sensible way to make a living.

How are ideas about wealth presented?

When Tubal tells Shylock about how Jessica has spent his money, he seems to care more about the money than his daughter. In court, he says that taking away his property is the same as taking away his life.

If Shylock thinks too much of money, perhaps Bassanio thinks too little. He has 'disabled' his **estate**. However, he borrows more money in the hope of marrying a rich woman, so he clearly is interested in money: he is just extravagant with it.

This attitude might seem irresponsible, especially as Bassanio puts Antonio's life at risk by accepting money from him. However, far from being punished for his extravagance, Bassanio is rewarded with a rich wife.

The choosing of the caskets presents an ambiguous attitude to wealth. In the gold casket, Morocco finds a **'memento mori'**, which tells us that wealth is pointless. The 'grinning idiot' in the silver casket suggest that pursuing money is foolish. Yet, **ironically**, the man who chooses the lead casket is rewarded with great wealth.

Key Quotations to Learn

Shylock: 'This was a way to thrive, and he was blest, / And thrift is blessing if men steal it not.' (Iiii)

Bassanio: 'Therefore, thou gaudy gold, / Hard food for Midas, I will none of thee,' (IIIii)

Shylock: 'You take my house when you do take the prop / That doth sustain my house. You take my life / When you do take the means whereby I live.' (IVi)

Summary

- The merchant Antonio and the money-lender Shylock are mutually dependent.
- Shylock is shown to be too fond of money but Bassanio wastes it.
- The casket scenes reveal an ambiguous attitude to wealth.

Sample Analysis

Bassanio's **anecdote** about shooting a second arrow after a lost one in his 'schooldays' implies that his plans are childish, confirmed by his reference to 'innocence'. This puts Antonio in the role of indulgent father, enabling his prodigality. Bassanio calls his plan a 'hazard', a risk or a gamble, and hopes to be 'fortunate', the **adjective** suggesting both hope and wealth. Antonio echoes this, saying his own 'fortunes are at sea', also playing on the double meaning of wealth and good luck. This suggests that sending Bassanio out to try his luck at Belmont is similar to sending his 'argosies' to trade around the world.

Questions

QUICK TEST
1. How do the Venetian Christians depend on the Jews?
2. What is thrift?
3. What is ironic about Bassanio's choice of casket?

EXAM PRACTICE
Using one or more of the 'Key Quotations to Learn', write a paragraph analysing how Shakespeare presents the theme of money.

Justice and Mercy

You must be able to: analyse how Shakespeare presents the themes of justice and mercy.

What ideas are presented about justice and mercy?

Justice is about fairness, doing what is morally right and upholding the law.
Mercy means showing compassion to those who have been defeated or have done something wrong.

How do characters present justice?

The Duke presides over the court, showing that justice comes from the state. However, he cannot change the laws of Venice.

Shylock pursues justice. He has a contract with Antonio and, because Antonio has not paid his debt on time, he can claim his 'forfeiture', the pound of flesh.

Portia's position in the court is ambiguous. She comes from Bellario as a legal adviser to the Duke, who allows her to act as a judge and decide on the legality of Shylock's claim. Later in the scene, she seems to be both judge and prosecutor.

Antonio submits to justice: he is willing to accept the court's ruling, offering his chest to be cut.

What sort of justice does the court dispense?

For dramatic effect, Shakespeare's court combines two functions, which would be dealt with separately in the English legal system.

The first part of Act 4 scene 1 deals with a 'civil' case, which has been brought by Shylock against Antonio. The court's job is to decide whether their contract is valid and Shylock can collect his pound of flesh.

In the second part of the scene, the court becomes a criminal court. Portia judges that Shylock has broken the law by seeking to kill Antonio and passes sentence on him.

How is mercy presented?

The Duke urges Shylock to show mercy to Antonio. Shylock refuses because he has made an oath, linking his pursuit of justice to his religion. He sees justice in terms of gaining revenge.

Portia argues that mercy 'blesseth him that gives and him that takes'. Her speech reflects Christian ideas about God's mercy. If we were judged strictly by God on our deeds, we would all be damned (and go to Hell) but God shows us mercy and saves us, so we can go to Heaven.

She asks Antonio and the Duke whether they will show mercy to Shylock. The Duke does so by not condemning him to death and charging a fine instead of taking half his property.

Whether Antonio is judged to show mercy depends on the audience's point of view. Many modern audiences and critics think his punishment is cruel, focussing on his conversion. However, Elizabethan audiences would probably have thought that Shylock was being shown mercy and offered salvation.

Key Quotations to Learn

Portia: 'The quality of mercy is not strained. / It droppeth like the gentle rain from heaven / Upon the place beneath:' (IVi)

Shylock: 'My deeds upon my head! I crave the law, / The penalty and forfeit of my bond.' (IVi)

Duke: 'Thou shalt see the difference of our spirit, / I pardon thee thy life before thou ask it:' (IVi)

Summary

- Justice is given out by the state but the Duke cannot change the law.
- Mercy comes from God and blesses both those who give it and those who receive it.
- The court changes from a civil court, with Shylock as complainant, to a criminal court, where he is the defendant.

Sample Analysis

Halfway through the court scene, Shakespeare pinpoints the moment of **peripeteia** when Shylock is about to cut into Antonio's flesh and Portia stops him with 'Tarry a while'. This pause at a moment of high tension freezes the action as she explains the letter of the law. Justice means he can take his 'pound of flesh' but not 'one drop of Christian blood'. Suddenly, both Shylock and Antonio undergo a reversal of fortune. The power shifts from Shylock to Antonio, Antonio escapes death and Shylock's life is in danger.

Questions

QUICK TEST
1. How is Portia's position in court ambiguous?
2. According to Portia, how does God show mercy?
3. How does the Duke show mercy?

EXAM PRACTICE
Using one or more of the 'Key Quotations to Learn', write a paragraph analysing how Shakespeare presents ideas about mercy.

Appearance and Reality

You must be able to: analyse how Shakespeare presents the theme of the difference between appearance and reality.

How does Shakespeare present the difference between appearance and reality?

Shakespeare uses two strong theatrical devices to explore ideas about what is real and what is not: disguise and the caskets.

How is disguise used?

A masque is an entertainment with music, with the performers often wearing masks. Being in disguise allows people to mix freely with members of the opposite sex and behave in ways that normally would not be allowed.

The men in the play are not really masquers but their disguise means that they can act outside society's conventions and help Lorenzo to elope with Jessica.

Jessica disguises herself as a page boy so she can escape from Venice. The male disguise gives her more freedom.

The **paradox** is that Lorenzo and Jessica have to disguise themselves to express their true feelings.

As Balthasar, Portia can express herself in a way that she could not if she were dressed as a woman.

Their disguises allow Portia and Nerissa to test their husbands' loyalty. The audience might question how real Bassanio and Gratiano's feelings are. Was the fairy-tale Belmont a place of illusion, where vows were made that cannot survive in the 'real' world of Venice? And how honest are the women if they feel the need to play tricks on their husbands?

How else are clothes used to explore appearance and reality?

The new liveries that Bassanio buys for his servants before leaving for Belmont are a sign of his extravagance and make him appear to be wealthy, when in fact he is in debt.

How are the caskets used?

The three caskets are used to show that it is a mistake to judge by outward appearance and that things that are valued in the world do not have real value.

The note in the golden casket states that 'all that glisters is not gold', meaning that not everything that looks valuable is valuable. The 'death', probably a skull, shows how unimportant gold is, as we will all die, regardless of wealth.

Arragon chooses the silver casket because of the motto saying he who chooses it will get what he deserves. He thinks he deserves Portia but inside the casket is a 'grinning idiot' showing that, in reality, he is a fool, as are all who pursue wealth.

Bassanio can see beyond the surface of the lead casket, not because he is clever but because he is in love with Portia. What is real is love, not wealth or power.

Key Quotations to Learn

Morocco: 'All that glisters is not gold;' (IIvii)

Bassanio: 'So may the outward shows be least themselves:' (IIIii)

Portia: '... in such a habit / That they shall think we are accomplished / With that we lack.' (IIIiv)

Summary

- Disguise gives the characters freedom to be themselves.
- Morocco and Arragon cannot see beyond outward show.
- Bassanio's love helps him see what is really valuable.

Sample Analysis

As an example of his assertion that 'the world is still deceived by ornament', Bassanio talks about men's cowardice being hidden by 'the beards of Hercules and frowning Mars', using the way in which the hero and the god of war are traditionally portrayed to provide a metaphor for deceit. He then moves on to women, using wigs ('the dowry of a second head') as a metaphor for deception and vanity. The idea that the hair in the wig has come from a dead woman recalls the 'carrion death' that Morocco found in the golden casket and underlines the worthlessness of human vanity.

Questions

QUICK TEST
1. What do the young men do under cover of the masque?
2. What does Arragon's choice show him to be?
3. What gives Bassanio the power to see beyond appearances?

EXAM PRACTICE
Using one or more of the 'Key Quotations to Learn', write a paragraph analysing how Shakespeare presents the theme of disguise.

Parents and Children

You must be able to: analyse how Shakespeare presents parents and children.

How is Portia's relationship with her father presented?

Portia has been 'richly left' following the death of her father but he still has control over her, influencing her choice of husband through the caskets. In this way, he continues to play the conventional role of the father in aristocratic or rich families.

The man who chooses correctly might do so because he is clever or just lucky, not because he is a suitable husband. However, this **motif** in the play comes from the tradition of myth and romance and should not be judged in practical terms. It is almost magical and is a way of judging whether a suitor truly loves Portia and is worthy of her.

Portia's father is a 'holy man', which makes the task also seem holy. Portia, despite some doubts, obeys his wishes, resisting the temptation to help Bassanio.

Her relationship with her dead father shows how a conventional father/daughter relationship should work.

How is Jessica and Shylock's relationship presented?

Jessica's relationship with Shylock contrasts with Portia and her father's. Jessica marries without her father's knowledge or consent. Rather than being given money, she steals it.

She is aware of her duty to her father, calling it a 'heinous sin' to be ashamed of him.

Shylock's attitude to Jessica is ambiguous. When he tells her to shut herself in the house, he could be seen either as **tyrannical** or as caring. When he hears of her elopement he is distressed, but focusses on the money she has taken. He wishes she were dead, which is shocking but also shows how much of a betrayal her marriage is.

Most audiences' sympathy would probably be with Jessica, as she is motivated by love. However, sympathies often shift to Shylock when he is told about her swapping a ring, presumably given to him by her mother, for a monkey. This makes her seems heartless and unfeeling towards her family.

How is the relationship between the Gobbos presented?

The Gobbos give an absurd, comic version of a parent/child relationship, which in some ways parallels Shylock and Jessica's relationship.

Old Gobbo does not recognise his son, which reflects Shylock's 'blindness' to what Jessica is doing. Launcelot pretends to be dead to get a reaction from his father; after her escape, Shylock talks about Jessica as if she were dead. Launcelot pretends to be someone else, causing distress to his father; Jessica pretends to be a boy to escape from her father.

Key Quotations to Learn

Nerissa: 'Your father was ever virtuous, and holy men at their deaths have good inspirations;' (Iii)

Jessica: 'Alack, what heinous sin it is in me / To be ashamed to be my father's child!' (IIiii)

Shylock (of Jessica): 'Would she were hearsed at my foot, and the ducats in her coffin!' (IIIi)

Summary

- Portia's father controls her after his death and she is obedient to him.
- Jessica, in contrast, betrays her father.
- Audience sympathies may shift between Jessica and Shylock.
- The Gobbos provide a comic counterpoint to Jessica and Shylock.

Sample Analysis

Although Jessica describes her home as 'hell', Shylock's attitude to her in their only scene together does not suggest that he is a cruel or tyrannical father, as he addresses her affectionately as 'Jessica, my girl'. He does not lock her in but hands her the keys to lock herself in, in his view keeping her safe from 'Christian fools'. This creates dramatic irony as the audience is aware of Lorenzo's plan to use a masque as a cover for their elopement. Far from keeping Jessica away from Christians, handing her the keys has given her the means both to escape and to steal from him.

Questions

QUICK TEST
1. How does Portia's father assert control?
2. Which incident might shift the audience's sympathies for Jessica to Shylock?
3. How might Shylock be said to be 'blind'?

EXAM PRACTICE
Using one or more of the 'Key Quotations to Learn', write a paragraph analysing how Shakespeare presents relationships between fathers and their children.

Tips and Assessment Objectives

You must be able to: understand how to approach the exam question and meet the requirements of the mark scheme.

Quick Tips

- You will get one question about a character or a theme. It will ask you to respond to a short extract from the play and to link your ideas to other scenes in *The Merchant of Venice*.

- Make sure you know what the question is asking you. Underline key words and pay particular attention to the bullet point prompts that come with the question.

- You should spend approximately 50 minutes on your response. Allow yourself between five and ten minutes to annotate the extract and plan your answer so there is some structure to your essay.

- All your paragraphs should contain a clear idea, a relevant reference to the play (ideally a quotation) and analysis of how Shakespeare conveys this idea. Whenever possible, you should link your comments to the play's context.

- It can sometimes help, after each paragraph, to quickly re-read the question to keep yourself focussed on the exam task.

- Keep your writing concise. If you waste time 'waffling' you won't be able to include the full range of analysis and understanding that the mark scheme requires.

- It is a good idea to remember what the mark scheme is asking of you …

AO1: Understand and respond to the play (12 marks)

This is all about coming up with a range of points that match the question, supporting your ideas with references from the play and writing your essay in a mature, academic style.

Lower	Middle	Upper
The essay has some good ideas that are mostly relevant. Some quotations and references are used to support the ideas.	A clear essay that always focusses on the exam question. Quotations and references support ideas effectively. The response refers to different points in the play.	A convincing, well-structured essay that answers the question fully. Quotations and references are well-chosen and integrated into sentences. The response covers the whole play (not everything, but ideas from the extract and a range of other Acts).

AO2: Analyse effects of Shakespeare's language, form and structure (12 marks)

You need to comment on how specific words, language techniques, sentence structures or the narrative structure allow Shakespeare to get his ideas across to the audience. This could simply be something about a character or a larger idea he is exploring through the play. To achieve this, you will need to have learned good quotations to analyse.

Lower	Middle	Upper
Identification of some different methods used by Shakespeare to convey meaning. Some subject terminology.	Explanation of Shakespeare's different methods. Clear understanding of the effects of these methods. Accurate use of subject terminology.	Analysis of the full range of Shakespeare's methods. Thorough exploration of the effects of these methods. Accurate range of subject terminology.

AO3: Understand the relationship between the play and its contexts (6 marks)

For this part of the mark scheme, you need to show your understanding of how the characters or Shakespeare's ideas relate to when he was writing (1590s) or where the play is set (Venice).

Lower	Middle	Upper
Some awareness of how ideas in the play link to its context.	References to relevant aspects of context show a clear understanding.	Exploration is linked to specific aspects of the play's contexts to show a detailed understanding.

AO4: Written accuracy (4 marks)

You need to use accurate vocabulary, expression, punctuation and spelling. Although it is only four marks, this could make the difference between a lower or a higher grade.

Lower	Middle	Upper
Reasonable level of accuracy. Errors do not get in the way of the essay making sense.	Good level of accuracy. Vocabulary and sentences help to keep ideas clear.	Consistent high level of accuracy. Vocabulary and sentences are used to make ideas clear and precise.

1. Read the following extract from Act 1 scene 3 and then answer the question that follows.

SHYLOCK	Well then, now it appears you need my help. Go to then. You come to me and you say 'Shylock, we would have moneys,' you say so, You, that did void your rheum upon my beard And foot me as you spurn a stranger cur Over your threshold, moneys is your suit What should I say to you? Should I not say, 'Hath a dog money? Is it possible A cur can lend three thousand ducats?' Or Shall I bend low, and in a bondman's key, With bated breath and whispering humbleness, Say this: 'Fair sir, you spat on me on Wednesday last, You spurned me such a day, another time You called me dog, and for these courtesies I'll lend you thus much moneys'?
ANTONIO	I am as like to call thee so again, To spit on thee again, to spurn thee too.

Starting with this extract, explore how Shakespeare presents the relationship between Shylock and Antonio. Write about:

- how Shakespeare presents their relationship in this extract
- how Shakespeare presents their relationship in the play as a whole.

2. Read the following extract from Act 3 scene 2 and then answer the question that follows.

PORTIA	I pray you tarry, pause a day or two Before you hazard, for in choosing wrong I lose your company. Therefore forbear a while. There's something tells me, but it is not love, I would not lose you: and you know yourself Hate counsels not in such a quality. But lest you should not understand me well – And yet a maiden hath no tongue but thought – I would retain you here some month or two Before you venture for me. I could teach you How to choose right, but then I am forsworn. So will I never be. So you may miss me.

Starting with this speech, how does Shakespeare present Portia in the play? Write about:

- how Shakespeare presents Portia in this speech
- how Shakespeare presents Portia in the play as a whole.

3. Read the following extract from Act 4 scene 1 and then answer the question that follows.

BASSANIO	Good sir, this ring was given me by my wife, And when she put it on she made me vow That I should neither sell nor give nor lose it.
PORTIA	That 'scuse serves many men to save their gifts, And if your wife be not a madwoman. And know how well I have deserved this ring, She would not hold out enemy for ever For giving it to me. Well, peace be with you! *Exeunt Portia and Nerissa*
ANTONIO	My Lord Bassanio, let him have the ring. Let his deservings, and my love withal, Be valued 'gainst your wife's commandment.
BASSANIO	Go, Gratiano, run and overtake him, Give him the ring and bring him if thou canst Unto Antonio's house. Away, make haste!

Starting with this extract, explore how Shakespeare presents Bassanio in the play. Write about:

- how Shakespeare presents Bassanio in this extract
- how Shakespeare presents Bassanio in the play as a whole.

4. Read the following extract from Act 4 scene 1 and then answer the question that follows.

SHYLOCK	As there is no firm reason to be rendered Why he cannot abide a gaping pig, Why he a harmless necessary cat, Why he a woollen bagpipe, but of force, Must yield to such inevitable shame As to offend, himself being offended; So can I give no reason, nor will I not, More than a lodged hate and a certain loathing I bear Antonio, that I follow thus A losing suit against him. Are you answered?
BASSANIO	This is no answer, thou unfeeling man, To excuse the current of thy cruelty.
SHYLOCK	I am not bound to please thee with my answers.
BASSANIO	Do all men kill the things they do not love?
SHYLOCK	Hates any man the thing he would not kill?
BASSANIO	Every offence is not a hate at first.
SHYLOCK	What, wouldst thou have a serpent sting thee twice?

Starting with this conversation, explain how far you think Shakespeare presents Shylock as a villain. Write about:

- how Shakespeare presents Shylock in this conversation
- how Shakespeare presents Shylock in the play as a whole.

Planning a Character Question Response

You must be able to: understand what an exam question is asking you and prepare your response.

How might an exam question on character be phrased?

A typical character question will read like this:

Read the following extract from Act 4 scene 1 and then answer the question that follows.

For the extract, see page 59.

Starting with this extract, explore how Shakespeare presents Bassanio in the play. Write about:

- how Shakespeare presents Bassanio in this extract
- how Shakespeare presents Bassanio in the play as a whole.

[30 marks + 4 AO4 marks]

How do I work out what to do?

The focus of this question is clear: the character of Bassanio.

The extract is your starting point. What does it tell you about Bassanio and how is this conveyed?

'How' is the key aspect of this question.

For AO1, you need to display a clear understanding of what Bassanio is like and his function in the play.

For AO2, you need to analyse the different ways in which Shakespeare's use of language, structure and the dramatic form help to show the audience what Bassanio is like. Ideally, you should include quotations that you have learnt but, if necessary, you can make a clear reference to a specific part of the play.

You also need to remember to link your comments to the play's context to achieve your AO3 marks and write accurately to pick up your four AO4 marks for spelling, punctuation and grammar.

How can I plan my essay?

You have approximately 50 minutes to write your essay.

This isn't long but you should spend the first 5 to 10 minutes reading and annotating the extract then writing a quick plan. This will help you to focus your thoughts and produce a well-structured essay.

Try to come up with three or four ideas from the extract and think how these can be developed using other parts of the play. Each of these ideas can then be written up as a paragraph.

You can write your points about the extract, followed by your exploration of the rest of the play. Or you can alternate your points between the extract and the rest of the play. Choose a method that best matches the question.

You can plan in whatever way you find most useful. Some students like to just make a quick list of points and then re-number them into a logical order. Spider diagrams are particularly popular. Look at the example below.

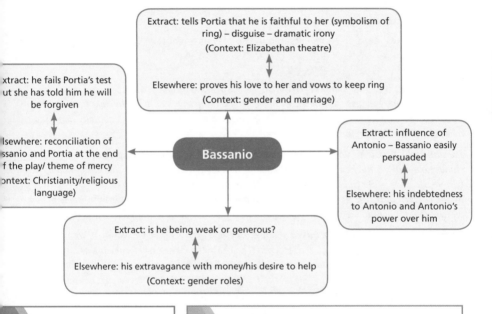

Extract: tells Portia that he is faithful to her (symbolism of ring) – disguise – dramatic irony
(Context: Elizabethan theatre)

Elsewhere: proves his love to her and vows to keep ring
(Context: gender and marriage)

Extract: he fails Portia's test but she has told him he will be forgiven

Elsewhere: reconciliation of Bassanio and Portia at the end of the play/ theme of mercy
(Context: Christianity/religious language)

Bassanio

Extract: influence of Antonio – Bassanio easily persuaded

Elsewhere: his indebtedness to Antonio and Antonio's power over him

Extract: is he being weak or generous?

Elsewhere: his extravagance with money/his desire to help
(Context: gender roles)

Summary

- Make sure you know what the focus of the essay is.
- Remember to analyse how ideas are conveyed by Shakespeare.
- Try to relate your ideas to the play's social and historical context.

Questions

QUICK TEST

1. What key skills do you need to show in your answer?

2. What are the benefits of quickly planning your essay?

3. Why is it better to have learned quotations for the exam?

EXAM PRACTICE

Plan a response to Question 1 on page 58.

Grade 5 Annotated Response

Read the following extract from Act 4 scene 1 and then answer the question that follows.

For the extract, see page 59.

Starting with this extract, explore how Shakespeare presents Bassanio in the play. Write about:

- how Shakespeare presents Bassanio in this extract
- how Shakespeare presents Bassanio in the play as a whole. [30 marks + 4 AO4 marks]

In this extract, Bassanio is talking to Portia, who is dressed as a boy, after the trial scene. It is dramatic irony because the audience knows he is talking to his wife but he does not (1). The Elizabethans would have thought it funnier because they knew the girl was actually being played by a boy (2). She asks him for his ring.

Bassanio tells Portia his wife 'made me vow/That I should neither sell nor give nor lose it'. This shows how important the ring is as a symbol of their love. It is a reminder that he should be faithful to her (3). He is polite to Portia, calling her 'Good Sir' but he seems very determined. Which is shown by the pattern of three: 'neither sell nor give nor lose it'. However, he says his wife 'made me vow', which makes it sound like she is in charge and he might not be as bothered as she is (4).

At the beginning of the play he talked about marrying Portia as if he was doing it because she was rich. He called her the 'golden fleece'. However, he chose the right casket, which was a symbol of him truly loving her. Still, the audience might think she loved him more as she said more about her feelings (5). Women then had to give all their property to their husbands when they got married so the audience might still think he is not as sincere as her (6). Maybe this is why she has to test him.

It looks as if he has passed the test. However, as soon as she has gone, Antonio persuades Bassanio to give away the ring. He says that Portia has earned it, 'his deservings', but also mentions 'my love withal' (7). He talks about Portia as if she was just being bossy saying 'your wife's commandment', as if it was just something she told him to do and not a vow. He is making his love more important than Portia's and it works because Bassanio changes his mind (8).

Antonio loves Bassanio and has offered his 'flesh' for him when he made his bond with Shylock. Bassanio wanted to return to Venice when he heard Antonio was in trouble, even though he had just got married. Portia supported him. However, now Antonio is asking him to put him before his wife and break a vow. It looks like Antonio has more power over him than Portia or that his love for Antonio is stronger than his love for Portia (9).

This shows that Bassanio is a weak character. As a wife, Portia was supposed to obey her husband but words like 'made' and 'commandment' make it seem like she is the strong one (10). Antonio is also stronger than Bassanio because Bassanio does whatever he wants. On the other hand, maybe Bassanio is being generous. After what Portia has done in the trial she has 'deserved this ring' and it looks mean not to give it to her. Bassanio has always been extravagant with money, which is why he needed to marry Portia (11).

At the end of the play, Portia forgives him and he makes another vow. There has got to be a happy ending, with everything sorted out because it is a comedy (12). Also, Portia has talked a lot about mercy so she has to show forgiveness herself. However, the audience might still think he is unreliable and weak, and that his love is not as strong as hers (13).

1. The essay starts with a clear summary of the situation in the extract, referring to the writer's methods and using appropriate terminology. AO1/AO2

2. Understanding of context shown but it is not linked to the question. AO3

3. Shakespeare's methods considered using appropriate terminology, backed by quotation. AO1/AO2

4. More clear explanation, using embedded quotations and relevant terminology but lacking analysis. AO1/AO2

5. Explanation of Bassanio's feeling and motivation. Clear references to other parts of the play. AO1

6. Some context is included but it isn't fully linked to the analysis. AO3

7. The essay refers to other parts of the play but tends to 'story-telling' with little or no analysis. AO1

8. A clear point made, based on textual reference. The language is a bit too informal for an exam essay. AO1/AO4

9. Makes a valid point about Bassanio's relationships but still tends towards story-telling rather than analysis. When writing about the play as a whole, this candidate has not paid enough attention to AO2. AO1

10. Quotations used effectively to demonstrate understanding of Shakespeare's use of language. Linked to context. AO1/AO3

11. Shows awareness of possible different interpretations, although a little vague. AO1/AO3

12. Clear link to context. AO3

13. Conclusion looks a little bit rushed, although it makes a clear point. AO1

Questions

EXAM PRACTICE

Choose a paragraph of this essay. Read it through a few times then try to rewrite and improve it. You might:

- Improve the sophistication of the language or the clarity of expression.
- Replace a reference with a quotation or use a better quotation.
- Ensure quotations are embedded in the sentence.
- Provide more detailed, or a wider range of, analysis.
- Use more subject terminology.
- Link some context to the analysis more effectively.

Grade 7+ Annotated Response

Read the following extract from Act 4 scene 1 and then answer the question that follows.

For the extract, see page 59.

Starting with this extract, explore how Shakespeare presents Bassanio in the play. Write about:

- how Shakespeare presents Bassanio in this extract
- how Shakespeare presents Bassanio in the play as a whole.   [30 marks + 4 AO4 marks]

After the tension of the trial scene, the play's focus has shifted to the relationship between Portia and Bassanio. In this extract, Portia's disguise enables her to speak freely as well as providing dramatic irony: the audience is aware not only of her identity as Bassanio's wife but also of her true purpose in asking for the ring (1).

*The ring is traditionally a symbol of love and fidelity, particularly in marriage (2). Bassanio recalls that Portia, his wife, 'made me vow/That I should neither sell nor give nor lose it'. This pattern of three **parallel phrases** suggests certainty and determination, reinforced by the triple negative of 'neither ... nor ... nor' (3). He appears at this point, to his wife and the audience, to be faithful. However, his use of the **verb** 'made' might suggest that his vow is an obligation rather than something entered into freely and there is no mention of love (4).*

At the start of the play he describes his courtship of Portia as part business venture, to 'get clear' of all his debts, and part 'hazard'. His comparison of her to the 'golden fleece' reinforces the idea that he is motivated by her wealth. However, by citing the story of Jason, he casts himself as an adventurer and lover as well as a treasure-hunter. In the next scene, Portia remembers him as a 'soldier and scholar', supporting this idea (5). This suggests mixed motives but, if love is not his only reason for marrying, he has qualities that fit him for the myth-like task ahead. When he chooses the correct casket, a powerful visual symbol of what is true and what is not, he proves that he loves Portia and is worthy of her love. Nevertheless, doubt about the strength of his love might linger, as Portia has given herself and her property entirely to him, as an Elizabethan woman would have to, and he has offered nothing in return (6). Maybe this is why she has to test him.

*When 'Balthasar' fails to persuade him to part with the ring, Bassanio appears to have passed the test. However, Antonio immediately tries to change his mind. First, he mentions Portia's 'deservings', recalling Portia's own argument in her previous speech. He then speaks of his 'love', which he says should be 'valued 'gainst your wife's commandment' (7). His use of the **abstract noun** 'commandment' suggests that Bassanio is under Portia's control, reversing the norm in society. It also has religious **connotations**, reminding the audience of the sacredness of marriage (8). This is not the first time Bassanio has done Antonio's bidding. When Antonio asks to see him before he dies, Bassanio goes immediately to Venice, showing love and loyalty to his friend but* *leaving his new wife behind. Antonio is now asking Bassanio to put his love and obligation to him in the balance with his love and duty to his wife, thereby breaking a vow he has made to her. Bassanio obeys him (9).*

This could be interpreted as showing that Bassanio is a weak character: Portia is the stronger partner in their marriage and Antonio is the stronger partner in their friendship. On the other hand, Bassanio's actions might be seen as those of a generous, open man who tries to do the right thing and please those whom he loves. Certainly, Portia has 'deserved this ring' – both as a lawyer and as a wife – and perhaps she means it when she says that his wife 'will not hold out enemy forever' (10).

At the end of the play, Portia does forgive him. Theatrical convention demands a happy ending and the lovers must be reconciled (11). Audiences might still think that Bassanio is unreliable and weak, but they might also recall that he has been referred to previously as 'prodigal' because of his extravagance and directly compared to the prodigal son of the parable. Mercy is a major theme of the play, called by Portia 'an attribute of God himself', so perhaps it is fitting that the play ends with her showing mercy to her own prodigal husband (12).

1. The essay starts with a clear summary of the situation in the extract, showing understanding of the play's structure, referring to the writer's methods and using accurate terminology. AO1/AO2

2. Accurate terminology. Understanding of context shown. AO2/AO3

3. Close analysis of Shakespeare's use of language, based on a well-chosen quotation and using appropriate terminology. AO1/AO2

4. An interesting idea based on close-reading, but not developed. AO1/AO2

5. Effective use of short quotations from elsewhere in the play, supporting a thoughtful response to the question about Bassanio's character. AO1/AO2

6. Ideas about the character's motivation developed further. Shows understanding and appreciation of Shakespeare's methods, using accurate terminology. Ideas linked to context. AO1/AO2/AO3

7. Effective use of embedded quotations. AO1/AO4

8. Analysis of language, effectively linked to specific aspects of the play's contexts. AO2/AO3

9. Exploration of Bassanio's relationships and what they say about his character. AO1

10. Exploration of ambiguity/possible different interpretations. AO1/AO3

11. Clear link to context. AO3

12. Conclusion links ideas to context and shows understanding of Shakespeare's methods. The question about Bassanio's character has been answered fully in a coherent essay, with a high level of written accuracy. AO1/AO2/AO3/AO4

Questions

EXAM PRACTICE
Spend approximately 50 minutes writing an answer to Question 1 on page 58.
Remember to use the plan you have already prepared.

1. Read the following extract from Act 3 scene 1 and then answer the question that follows.

SHYLOCK:	Why there, there, there, there! A diamond gone cost me two thousand ducats in Frankfurt! The curse never fell upon our nation until now; I never felt it till now. Two thousand ducats in that, and other precious, precious jewels. I would my daughter were dead at my foot, and the jewels in her ear! Would she were hearsed at my foot, and the ducats in her coffin! No news of them, why so? – And I know not what's spent in the search. Why thou loss upon loss! The thief gone with so much, and so much to find the thief! – and no satisfaction, no revenge! Nor no ill luck stirring but what lights o'my shoulders, no sighs but o'my breathing, no tears but o'my shedding.

Starting with this speech, how does Shakespeare present attitudes to money and wealth in the play? Write about:

- how Shakespeare presents attitudes to money and wealth in this extract
- how Shakespeare presents attitudes to money and wealth in the play as a whole.

2. Read the following extract from Act 4 scene 1 and then answer the question that follows.

PORTIA:	The quality of mercy is not strained, It droppeth as the gentle rain from heaven Upon the place beneath. It is twice blest, It blesseth him that gives and him that takes. 'Tis mightiest in the mightiest, it becomes The throned monarch better than his crown. His sceptre shows the force of temporal power, The attribute to awe and majesty, Wherein doth sit the dread and fear of kings; But mercy is above this sceptred sway, It is enthroned in the hearts of kings, It is an attribute to God himself, And earthly power doth then show likest God's When mercy seasons justice. Therefore, Jew, Though justice be thy plea, consider this: That in the course of justice none of us Should see salvation. We do pray for mercy, And that same prayer doth teach us all to render The deeds of mercy.

Starting with this extract, explore how Shakespeare presents the theme of mercy. Write about:

- how Shakespeare presents the theme of mercy in this extract
- how Shakespeare presents the theme of mercy in the play as a whole.

3. Read the following extract from Act 4 scene 1 and then answer the question that follows.

BASSANIO:	Why dost thou whet thy knife so earnestly?
SHYLOCK:	To cut the forfeiture from that bankrupt there.
GRATIANO:	Not on thy sole, but on thy soul, harsh Jew, Thou mak'st they knife keen; but no metal can, No, no hangman's axe, bear half the keenness Of thy sharp envy. Can no prayers pierce thee?
SHYLOCK:	No, none that thou hast wit enough to make.
GRATIANO:	O be thou damned, inexecrable dog, And for thy life let justice be accused! Thou almost mak'st me waver in my faith, To hold opinion with Pythagoras That souls of animals infuse themselves Into the trunks of men. Thy currish spirit Governed by a wolf who, hanged for human slaughter, Even from the gallows did his fell soul fleet, And whilst thou layest in thy unhallowed dam, Infused itself in thee; for thy desires Are wolvish, bloody, starved, and ravenous.

Starting with this extract, how does Shakespeare present hatred and prejudice? Write about:

• how Shakespeare presents hatred and prejudice in this extract
• how Shakespeare presents hatred and prejudice in the play as a whole.

4. Read the following extract from Act 3 scene 2 and then answer the question that follows.

BASSANIO:	Madam, you have bereft me of all words. Only my blood speaks to you in my veins, And there is such confusion in my powers As, after some oration fairly spoke By a beloved prince, there doth appear Among the buzzing pleased multitude, Where every something being blent together Turns to a wild of nothing, save of joy Expressed and not expressed. But when this ring Part from my finger, then parts life from hence. O, then be bold to say Bassanio's dead.

Starting with this speech, explore how Shakespeare presents love and marriage. Write about:

• how Shakespeare presents love and marriage in this speech
• how Shakespeare presents love and marriage in the play as a whole.

Planning a Theme Question Response

You must be able to: understand what an exam question is asking you and prepare your response.

How might an exam question on theme be phrased?

A typical theme question will read like this:

Read the following extract from Act 4 scene 1 and then answer the question that follows.

For the extract, see page 67.

Starting with this extract, how does Shakespeare present hatred and prejudice? Write about:

- how Shakespeare presents hatred and prejudice in this extract
- how Shakespeare presents hatred and prejudice in the play as a whole.

[30 marks + 4 AO4 marks]

How do I work out what to do?

The focus of this question is clear: hatred and prejudice.

The extract is your starting point. Think about who hates whom, who is prejudiced, why they feel like this and how these feelings are presented.

'How' is the key aspect of this question.

For AO1, you need to display a clear understanding of which characters show hatred and prejudice, why they feel the way they do and where this is shown in the play.

For AO2, you need to analyse the different ways in which Shakespeare's use of language, structure and the dramatic form help to show hatred and prejudice. Ideally, you should include quotations that you have learnt but, if necessary, you can make a clear reference to a specific part of the play.

You also need to remember to link your comments to the play's context to achieve your AO3 marks and write accurately to pick up your four AO4 marks for spelling, punctuation and grammar.

How can I plan my essay?

You have approximately 50 minutes to write your essay.

This isn't long but you should spend the first 5 to 10 minutes reading and annotating the extract then writing a quick plan. This will help you to focus your thoughts and produce a well-structured essay.

Try to come up with three or four ideas from the extract and think how these can be developed using other parts of the play. Each of these ideas can then be written up as a paragraph.

You can write your points about the extract, followed by your exploration of the rest of the play. Or you can alternate your points between the extract and the rest of the play. Choose a method that best matches the question.

You can plan in whatever way you find most useful. Some students like to just make a quick list of points and then re-number them into a logical order. Spider diagrams are particularly popular; look at the examples below.

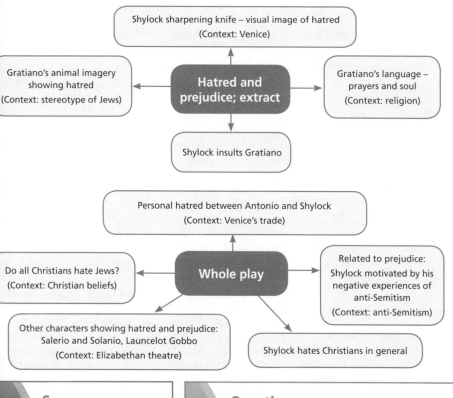

Summary

- Make sure you know what the focus of the essay is.
- Remember to analyse how ideas are conveyed by Shakespeare.
- Try to relate your ideas to the play's social and historical context.

Questions

QUICK TEST
1. What key skills do you need to show in your answer?
2. What are the benefits of quickly planning your essay?
3. Why is it better to have learned quotations for the exam?

EXAM PRACTICE
Plan a response to Question 1 on page 66.

Grade 5 Annotated Response

Read the following extract from Act 4 scene 1 and then answer the question that follows.

For the extract, see page 67.

Starting with this extract, how does Shakespeare present hatred and prejudice?
Write about:

- how Shakespeare presents hatred and prejudice in this extract
- how Shakespeare presents hatred and prejudice in the play as a whole.

[30 marks + 4 AO4 marks]

*The extract starts with Shylock sharpening his knife. This shows that he is keen to cut out Antonio's flesh and shows how much he hates him (1). Shylock's reply to Bassanio refers to the deal between him and Antonio, the 'forfeiture'. It reminds the audience that the argument is about money and trade, which is important in Venice (2). The **noun** 'bankrupt' sounds insulting and shows that Shylock hates Antonio personally because of his business dealings. It sounds a bit like he is spitting (3).*

Gratiano makes a pun on the words 'soul' and 'sole', making reference to religion and inferring that what Shylock is doing is a sin (4). He calls him 'harsh Jew', which makes us think he dislikes him not just because of what he is doing but because of his being a Jew, which shows prejudice (5). He accuses Shylock of 'sharp envy', comparing its strength to a hangman's axe. Cutting people's heads off with an axe was a common way of executing them in Elizabethan times (6).

Shylock replies by saying Gratiano is stupid. This makes Gratiano react with hatred. He tells him to be 'damned', which is very serious and picks up on what he said about his 'soul'. Christians would think Jews would be damned anyway so it also shows prejudice (7). Gratiano calls Shylock an 'inexecrable dog', a metaphor that shows hatred and prejudice because it is like he is saying Jews are not human. It is an insult that Antonio and other characters have used before (8). He goes on to talk about animals' souls going into humans. He says Shylock is a wolf and at the end of his speech he uses four strong adjectives to describe him, 'wolvish, bloody, starved and ravenous'. This language is very violent and shows a lot of hatred (9).

From the start of the play, Antonio and Shylock hate each other. Antonio says it is because Shylock does not like him lending money and not charging interest, ruining Shylock's business. Shylock can lend money because he is a Jew so Christians depend on him. He is important to Venice's trade (10). However, there is a lot of anti-Semitic prejudice from Antonio. Shylock complains that Antonio spat on him and kicked him just because he is Jewish and Antonio says he would do it again (11).

Other characters also show anti-Jewish prejudice, including Salerio and Solanio when they call Shylock 'dog' and laugh about him being upset. Launcelot Gobbo thinks Shylock is a 'devil' but his prejudice is shown in a comic way because he is the clown. There was usually a clown in Shakespeare's plays and when he says things the audience think they are ridiculous. However, the other characters who hate Jews are typical of people in Venice and in England at the time (12).

This makes Shylock hate Antonio and want to have his 'pound of flesh'. Shylock also says bad things about Christians in general, showing there is hate on both sides (13). It is hard to say whether all

Christians in the play hate Jews. Portia and Bassanio do not use bad language to Shylock, although Portia calls him 'Jew'. The audience might think they all hate Jews because they make Shylock become Christian but in Elizabethan times, people would have thought this was a good thing because it would save his soul (14).

1. The opening sentence refers to the text and makes a point that is focussed on the question. AO1

2. Some contextual understanding linked to the text but the point made is not linked to the question. AO3

3. Relevant quotation and simple subject terminology is used; the effect of the use of the word is explained clearly. AO1/AO2

4. Reasonable attempt at explaining the effect of Shakespeare's use of language. Misuse of 'inferring'. AO2/AO4

5. Relevant point made, based on a well-chosen quotation, though not analysed. AO1

6. Quotation linked to context but its relevance to the question is not very clear. AO3

7. Better focus on the question as a new point is made and linked to context. AO1/AO3

8. Explanation of Shakespeare's use of language, using appropriate terminology. There is a relevant reference to another part of the play. AO1/AO2

9. Develops the point made above. Uses relevant quotation and comments on its effect but is lacking in analysis. AO1/AO2

10. The candidate moves on to the play as a whole. Relevant point made about an aspect of 'hate' (how far is it personal?), linked to context. Written expression lacks clarity. AO1/AO3/AO4

11. Still focussing on the question, considers another aspect of hate and prejudice. Comments rather undeveloped but there is a clear reference to the text. AO1/AO2

12. Develops the point about prejudice, referring to other parts of the play. Comments linked to contexts. AO1/AO3

13. Another reasonable point focussed on the question. Lacks detail and analysis, as does most of the commentary on 'the play as a whole'. AO1.

14. A considered response to conclude, showing understanding of context. The essay lacks the coherence and sophistication, as well as the analysis, necessary for a high mark. AO1/AO3/AO4

Questions

EXAM PRACTICE

Choose a paragraph of this essay. Read it through a few times then try to rewrite and improve it. You might:

- Improve the sophistication of the language or the clarity of expression.
- Replace a reference with a quotation or use a better quotation.
- Ensure quotations are embedded in the sentence.
- Provide more detailed, or a wider range of, analysis.
- Use more subject terminology.
- Link some context to the analysis more effectively.

Grade 7+ Annotated Response

Read the following extract from Act 4 scene 1 and then answer the question that follows.
For the extract, see page 67.

Starting with this extract, how does Shakespeare present hatred and prejudice? Write about:

- how Shakespeare presents hatred and prejudice in this extract
- how Shakespeare presents hatred and prejudice in the play as a whole.

[30 marks + 4 AO4 marks]

The powerful image of Shylock sharpening his knife shows his blood-thirsty hatred for Antonio. This image of hatred might inspire hatred for Shylock in the audience (1). Shylock's reference to Antonio as a 'bankrupt' expresses contempt for his failure in business, reminding us of the central role played by trade in the life of Venice (2). The noun 'bankrupt' reduces Antonio in status and its combination of plosives make it sound almost as if Shylock is spitting on Antonio, just as Shylock was spat on in the past (3).

*Gratiano's language in the following speech does not overtly express hatred or prejudice but there is an implied dislike of Shylock and Jews in general (4). His pun on the words 'soul' and 'sole' suggests that Shylock is sinful. His juxtaposition of the adjective 'harsh' with the proper noun 'Jew' implies that the two words belong together, suggesting that he expects harshness from a Jew, as he might expect him to care little about his soul (5). He accuses Shylock of 'sharp envy', implying that he is not driven by justice but by a deadly sin, which Christians at the time would expect from a Jew. His **rhetorical question**, 'Can no prayers pierce thee?' clearly expects the answer 'no' (6).*

*Shylock's response, suggesting Gratiano has no 'wit', provokes an aggressive speech. Gratiano tells him to be 'damned' and refers to his 'unhallowed dam', reflecting the belief that Jews could not be saved and attain Heaven unless they converted to Christianity (7). He calls Shylock an 'inexecrable dog', a metaphor used previously by Antonio and others and linked to Shylock's Jewishness, implying that Jews are less than human (8). He develops this idea by theorising that Shylock has the soul of a wolf 'hanged for human slaughter', which has connotations of witchcraft and macabre practices of a kind that Jews were sometimes accused of. He ends his speech with four **emotive** adjectives, 'wolvish, bloody, starved and ravenous', which convey both his hatred of Shylock and his perception of Shylock's hatred of Antonio (9).*

From the start of the play, Antonio and Shylock express hatred for each other. Both claim that their enmity is personal. Antonio has been lending money without charging interest, thereby potentially ruining Shylock's business. To Christians, 'usury' is a sin. However, the trade of Venice depends on borrowed money and is therefore dependent on Jews, who do not think charging interest is wrong (10). Antonio's hatred of Shylock, therefore, is linked to his Jewishness and the extent of his anti-Semitism is revealed when Shylock describes how Antonio spat on him and kicked him. Shylock poses the rhetorical question, 'What is his reason?' and answers it with 'I am a Jew' (11). Other characters also express hatred of Shylock, linked to prejudice, although not as violently. Solanio, representing the citizens of Venice, calls him 'dog' and compares him to the devil. Launcelot Gobbo also refers to him constantly as a 'devil'. All these characters have personal reasons for disliking Shylock, but their constant references to his Jewishness suggest that their hatred is partly based on prejudice (12).

Shylock, in turn, hates Antonio and is determined to get revenge for his treatment. Modern audiences' sympathies tend to lie with Shylock because of the prejudice against him but he too shows prejudice, calling Christians 'fools' and stating that he hates Antonio 'for he is a Christian'. Shakespeare shows hatred engenders more hatred (13).

Some people feel that the play itself is anti-Semitic, suggesting that Shakespeare is presenting his own prejudice. However, the impassioned speeches given to Shylock about being Jewish contradict this idea, while Launcelot's role as 'clown' causes ambiguity: perhaps it is his prejudice, not Shylock's religion, that is being ridiculed. Modern audiences are often shocked by Shylock's conversion to Christianity, feeling that this is an act of anti-Semitism. However, Elizabethan audiences would have seen it as an act of mercy and forgiveness, as saving his soul: the opposite of hatred. There is undoubtedly much hatred and prejudice presented in the play but how different audiences interpret what they see might be influenced their own prejudices (14).

1. The opening sentences refer to the text and make a point that is focussed on the question, using appropriate terminology and exploring the effect of the image. AO1/AO2
2. Contextual understanding linked to the text. AO3
3. Analysis of the effect of Shakespeare's use of language, using appropriate terminology. AO1/AO2
4. Clear focus on the question as the candidate moves to another point. AO1
5. Detailed analysis of language and its effect, linked to a reference to context. AO1
6. Develops point with further reference to context, supported by relevant quotations. AO1/AO3
7. Thoughtful consideration of the effects of language, linked to context and supported by relevant quotation. AO2/AO3
8. Explanation of Shakespeare's use of language, using appropriate terminology. There is a relevant reference to another part of the play. AO1/AO2
9. Develops the point made above, using relevant quotations and accurate terminology. Relates point to context and to the question about hatred. AO1/ AO2/AO3
10. The candidate moves on to the play as a whole. Relevant point made about the link between personal hatred and prejudice, linked to context. AO1/AO3
11. Develops a point about prejudice, supported by apt quotation and using accurate terminology. AO1/AO2
12. Expands the point about prejudice, referring to other parts of the play and other characters and showing understanding of the effects of the writer's methods. AO1/AO2
13. A new point exploring hatred and prejudice, linked to context, supported by a suitable quotation. AO/AO3.
14. A thoughtful concluding paragraph, showing understanding of contexts and different points of view, clearly focussed on the question. The essay has been coherent and the written expression accurate and clear throughout. AO1/AO3/AO4

Questions

EXAM PRACTICE

Spend approximately 50 minutes writing an answer to Question 1 on page 66.

Remember to use the plan you have already prepared.

Glossary

Abstract noun – a noun that is an idea or quality rather than a concrete object (such as: charity, compassion).

Active verb – a verb in the active voice, when the subject is the thing or person acting, for example, 'the dog bit the boy'.

Adjective – a word that describes a noun.

Alien – foreigner or stranger.

Alliteration (*adjective* alliterative) – a series of words beginning with the same sound.

Ambiguous – having more than one meaning, uncertain.

Anecdote – a brief story, used to illustrate a point.

Antipathy – strong dislike.

Anti-Semitism – prejudice against or hatred of Jewish people.

Argosy (*noun* argosies) – a large merchant ship.

Atmosphere – a tone, mood or general feeling.

Attitude – feeling about or opinion of something or someone.

Bond – a binding agreement/promise to pay borrowed money.

Caesuras – pause in a poetic line or a sentence.

Carrion – rotting (flesh).

Chorus – in drama (especially Greek drama), a group of people who comment on the action of the play.

City-state – an independent city with its own government.

Climax – the high point of a story, usually near the end.

Confidante – a trusted female friend who can be confided in (male equivalent is 'confidant').

Connotation – an implied meaning or something suggested by association.

Consummation – sexual intercourse after marriage that makes the marriage legal.

Convention – the established and accepted way of doing something.

Denouement – literally 'untying', the sorting out of a plot at the end of a play or story.

Derogatory – insulting, lowering.

Diction – choice of vocabulary.

Doctor – a well-educated person (not necessarily medical).

Dramatic irony – a situation in which the audience knows something that a character or characters do not.

Ducat – a gold coin.

Elope (*noun* elopement) – to run away from home with a lover.

Eloquence (*adjective* eloquent) – speaking fluently and well.

Emotive – creating or describing strong emotions.

Established church – the official church of a country, in England, the Church of England.

Estate – a person's property, often used of the property left by someone who has died.

Exposition – the opening part of a novel or play where setting and characters are introduced.

Fool – a silly person, sometimes employed by kings and others to entertain.

Heiress – a woman who has been or will be left property or money (male equivalent is 'heir').

Hunchback – a person with a hump on his/her back.

Hyperbole – exaggeration.

Hypocrisy – insincerity, especially saying one thing and doing another.

Image/Imagery – words used to create a picture in the imagination.

Imperative – an order or command.

Imply – to suggest something that is not expressly stated.

Innuendo – a hint.

Infer (*noun* inference) – to deduce something that is not openly stated.

Irony (*adjective* ironic; *adverb* ironically) – when words are used to imply an opposite meaning.

Jacob – in the Old Testament, the son of Isaac and grandson of Abraham.

Juxtaposition – the placing of two things (especially words) next to each other. Note that the use of this word does **not** necessarily imply contrast.

Kinsman – a relative (female equivalent is kinswoman').

Livery – a servant's uniform.

Masque – a musical entertainment, often with the performers wearing masks.

Masquer – someone who takes part in a masque.

Melancholy – habitual, thoughtful sadness.

Memento Mori – an object (such as a skull) kept as a reminder of death.

Metaphor – an image created by referring to something as something else.

Moses – in the Bible (the book of Exodus), the prophet who led the Israelites out of Egypt and received the Ten Commandments from God.

Motif – an idea or theme that recurs in a text.

Motivation – reason for doing something.

Norm – generally accepted standard of behaviour.

Noun – a naming word.

Overtly – openly or directly.

Parable – in the New Testament, a story told by Jesus with a moral or spiritual message.

Paradox – contradictory, apparently absurd, statement or situation.

Parallel phrasing – repeating the structure and some of the words in two or more phrases to make a pattern.

Peripeteia – sudden reversal of fortune.

Personification (*verb* personify) – writing about an idea or object as if it were human.

Pre-destination – the belief that our futures are mapped out and cannot be changed.

Prodigal Son – the subject of a parable in which a son wastes all the money that his father has given him but is welcomed back into the family home. The message is that God will forgive sinners.

Prop (short for 'property') – an object used in a stage production, including furniture.

Protagonist – the main character.

Publican – in the New Testament, a tax collector, generally hated by the Jewish people.

Rhetoric (*adjective* rhetorical) – the art of speaking.

Rhetorical question – a question that the speaker does not expect to be answered.

Significance – meaning, importance.

Simile – an image created by a comparison using the word 'as' or 'like'.

Stereotype – a person or thing conforms to a widely accepted (often derogatory) type.

Suitor – a man who is courting a woman with the aim of marrying her.

Superstition – irrational belief (usually in the supernatural).

Symbolise – (of an object) to represent a specific idea or meaning.

Synagogue – Jewish place of worship.

The Trojan War – in mythology, a long war fought between the Greeks and Trojans, involving a 10-year siege of the city of Troy.

Trust – a contract that makes someone the nominal owner of property to be used for someone else's benefit.

Turning point – a point in a story when things change significantly.

Tyrant (*adjective* tyrannical) – a cruel ruler.

Usury – lending money and charging interest. In modern usage, lending money and charging excessive interest.

Verb – a doing, feeling, thinking or being word.

Answers

Pages 4–5

Quick Test

1. Venice and Belmont.
2. To go to Belmont to woo (court) Portia.
3. Usury (lending money and charging interest).
4. A pound of flesh.

Exam Practice

Answers might include **exposition** of the relationship between Antonio and Bassanio, Bassanio's intention to court Portia, the establishment of Antonio's trading interests and Bassanio's wasting of money, the two settings established at the beginning of the first two scenes, exposition of Portia's situation in her conversation with Nerissa, introduction of Shylock and his relationship with Antonio and the **turning point** at the end of scene 3, leaving the audience anticipating the outcome of Bassanio's quest and Antonio's bond.

Analysis might include Shylock's focus on money and numbers ('three thousand ducats'), the importance of Portia being 'richly left', Bassanio's use of anecdote, the language of trade and commerce, careful explanation of the suitors' task, contrast in atmosphere between Venice and Belmont and the violent **diction** used by Shylock and Antonio.

Pages 6–7

Quick Test

1. Marry Lorenzo and convert to Christianity.
2. A page boy.
3. The golden one.
4. The silver one.

Exam Practice

Answers might focus on the sense of excitement and trickery created by the men dressing as masquers, dramatic irony created by the audience knowing Jessica's plans when Shylock does not, the sense of danger as Shylock might discover the plot, anticipation of what he might do when he finds Jessica gone, tension created by Morocco making his choice before Bassanio and the anticipation of what might be in the casket.

Analysis might include **hyperbole** used by Lorenzo of Jessica's qualities, comparison of Jessica and Portia's situations (references to 'father' and 'daughter'), Shylock's concern about Jessica being locked up and his use of the imperative, the use of the adjective 'good' to describe Antonio, the use of short scenes and the Gobbos used to release tension.

Pages 8–9

Quick Test

1. He is delighted and determined to pursue his bond.
2. The leaden one.
3. A ring.
4. Lorenzo and Jessica.

Exam Practice

Answers might include Antonio's need to pay Shylock and the nature of his bond, Shylock's opportunity to get revenge ('I'll have my bond'), Bassanio leaving Portia on his wedding day and the opportunity it gives to Portia to help Bassanio and to test his love. Analysis might include language used by Portia to express her love ('lord'), the use of classical references, Shylock's emotive language (repetition of 'I will'/ 'I'll'), other characters' anti-Semitic use of animal imagery and the significance of Portia and Nerissa dressing as men.

Pages 10–11

Quick Test

1. He hates him.
2. Portia disguised as a lawyer.
3. Jessica and Lorenzo.

Exam Practice

Answers could focus on the establishment of the situation, Shylock's entrance, the Duke and Bassanio's failure to persuade him to show mercy, Portia's entrance in disguise, her taking over of proceedings, the case apparently going Shylock's way, his sharpening of his knife, the visual image of Antonio baring his chest, the sudden change of fortunes (peripeteia) reflected in the use of caesura, with Shylock being under attack and building to a **climax** when he is sentenced and defeated.

Pages 12–13

Quick Test

1. Lovers from classical stories.
2. Belmont at night.
3. The ring that she had given Bassanio.
4. Some of his ships have arrived.

Exam Practice

Answers might focus on the atmosphere created in Jessica and Lorenzo's conversation ('In such a night'), their unsettling references to tragic lovers, their anticipation of Portia's return, the building of expectation in the audience, the confrontation about the rings and the way in which the women comically humiliate the men, Antonio's intervention, Portia's role in controlling the denouement and the way that Act 5 is sometimes seen as an anti-climax after the trial scene.

Pages 14–15

Quick Test

1. The Doge (Duke in the play).
2. Asia.
3. Lend money at interest.
4. Portia's.

Exam Practice

Answers might include the contrast with the busy city of Venice, the quiet nature of the first scene there, how it is a more 'female' place than Venice, the way the setting up of the task is reminiscent of classical myths or fairy tales, the use of references to myths, the building up of a magical/spiritual atmosphere through music and striking visual imagery, the gentle pace of the action, the description of the night and the candles in Act 5, and the way everything can be resolved there.

Pages 16–17

Quick Test

1. Under 200.
2. Roman Catholics.
3. The Torah.
4. Christianity.

Exam Practice

Answers might include the role of Jews in lending money and the Christian traders' dependency on them, the separate life led by Shylock and Jessica, distrust of Christians,

hylock's position as an 'alien', the constant references to his
ewishness, reference to the synagogue showing that he can
vorship freely, his apparently equal access to the law, casual
nti-Semitism, the wealth of Shylock and Tubal and references
o others 'of his tribe', indicating a sizeable community.
Answers might also include lack of clarity about why Shylock is
n 'alien' (because he is a Jew or was he born elsewhere?) and
o mention of the ghetto or curfew.

ages 18–19
Quick Test
. The Lord Chamberlain's Men.
. Richard Burbage, Will Kempe.
. Act 2 scene 7 (IIvii) (also IIix and IIIii).
xam Practice
Answers might include the 'flourish of cornets' to show the
ower of Morocco and formality of the occasion, probable
se of music as part of the masque, the song when Bassanio
hooses, the music played at the beginning of Act 5, its use
o create and heighten atmosphere, its use to enhance
neaning, ideas about love in song lyrics and its use to
ntertain and amuse.

ages 20–21
Quick Test
. Go to university/work as a doctor or
lawyer/act professionally.
. Widows or single women.
. She is 'marrying out' and becoming a Christian.
xam Practice
Answers might include Portia's unusual status in owning
roperty, her father's control of her, her willingness to obey
im despite doubts, Bassanio's motivation in courting her, the
act that he both loves her and gains from the marriage, the
ssumption that her property goes to him on marriage, her
ubmission to his authority, her use of words such as 'lord'
nd 'king', her comparison of her to a ruler, the delay in the
onsummation of the marriage, the importance of fidelity and
he symbolism of the ring.

ages 22–23
Quick Test
. Her father, the King of Troy.
. The Golden Fleece.
. Medea.
xam Practice
Answers might include Bassanio's references to Jason and the
olden Fleece, suggesting both his role as an adventurer and
ers as a prize, her comparison of him to the hero Hercules,
he implied idea that he is rescuing her, ambiguity implied
y the story of Medea and Jason, the implication that Portia's
ather has 'sacrificed' her and the significance of
ortia's name.

ages 24–25
Quick Test
. Jacob and Laban's sheep.
. Abraham's slave and the mother of his son, Ishmael.
. The parable of the prodigal son.

Exam Practice
Answers might include how Shylock's references to the Old
Testament identify his race and religion, his use of the Bible
to defend money lending, his use of biblical references to
insult other characters, the way in which his knowledge
might demonstrate his intelligence/cleverness, Antonio's
disagreement with Shylock about the meaning of a bible story,
references to New Testament teachings by Portia, Bassanio's
identification with the prodigal son, Launcelot Gobbo's comic
misinterpretation of the Bible and Shakespeare's assumption
that his audience would be familiar with the Bible.

Pages 26–27
Quick Test
1. Jessica.
2. Taunted him, kicked him and spat on him.
3. He refuses the money offered by Bassanio.
Exam Practice
Answers might include the verbal and physical abuse he has
received ('Thou call'dst me a dog'), his belief that Christians
are hypocritical, his resentment of Antonio lending money
without interest, his desire to keep his daughter away from
Christians, his hatred of Christians, his desire for revenge and
his determination to pursue his case. Analysis might include his
use of repetition ('An oath, an oath! I have an oath'), his use
of the animal imagery others have used against him ('But since
I am a dog, beware my fangs'), his use of rhetorical questions
to make other characters and the audience question their
feelings, the switch from verse to prose when he becomes
emotional and the symbolic importance of the 'pound
of flesh'.

Pages 28–29
Quick Test
1. He was wise and holy.
2. Dr Bellario.
3. Shylock.
Exam Practice
Answers might include the importance of her disguise, giving
her authority and the freedom to speak, the dramatic impact
of her entrance, her control of the scene, her knowledge of
the law and cleverness in interpreting it, her **rhetorical** skill,
her emphasis on mercy, her dual role as prosecutor and judge
and her attitude to Shylock and her motivation for being there.
Analysis might include her references to Christian teaching,
the **simile** she uses to describe mercy, the comparison of her to
Daniel and her use of questions and **imperatives**.

Pages 30–31
Quick Test
1. He is sad or melancholy.
2. Give the ring to Balthasar (Portia).
3. Merchant.
Exam Practice
Answers might include Antonio's claim to dislike Shylock
simply because of his profession, his assertion that Shylock
dislikes him because he lends money without interest, his
decision to ask Shylock for money despite this, Shylock's
revelation of Antonio's insulting and violent behaviour to
him, the sense that this comes from prejudice as much as

Answers

personal dislike, other characters' admiration of Antonio, his apparent change in attitude when Shylock lends him the money, his failed attempt to get Shylock not to pursue the bond and his acceptance of the verdict that he should pay with his flesh. Analysis might include Antonio's insulting language, including the use of animal imagery, the use of **active verbs** in Shylock's description of his behaviour, Shylock's description of him as a 'fawning publican' and his naivety/hypocrisy in calling Shylock 'kind'.

Pages 32–33
Quick Test
1. Antonio.
2. He is genuine and loves Portia.
3. By offering him money (more than he is owed).
Exam Practice
Answers might focus on his description of his intentions to Antonio as a gamble and an adventure, comparisons to Jason and Hercules, the fairy-tale or mythical nature of the task set by Portia's father, his status as a 'soldier and scholar' and his journey to Belmont to woo Portia and back to Venice to rescue Antonio. Analysis might include his use of the anecdote about the arrows, his use of the vocabulary of trade, the connotations of the references to mythical heroes and their stories, the build-up to his choice of casket, use of the metaphor 'rack' to imply suffering, Nerissa's hyperbolic praise of him, and the sense of risk reflected in the use of terms such as 'hazard' and 'lottery' to describe the task.

Pages 34–35
Quick Test
1. Waiting woman/companion.
2. Bassanio.
3. Portia.
4. Bassanio must choose the correct casket.
Exam Practice
Answers might focus on his function as Bassanio's companion, the way in which his story shadows Bassanio's, his characterisation of himself to Antonio, Bassanio's account of his character using three short adjectives ('Thou art too wild, too rude and bold of voice'), the suddenness of his revelation of his love for Nerissa, his behaviour in the trial scene and his part in the denouement. Analysis might include how he plays the 'fool', his talking to little purpose ('Gratiano speaks an infinite deal of nothing'), his use of innuendo, his derogatory language used to Shylock, his interjections in the court scene and use of exclamations.

Pages 36–37
Quick Test
1. Antonio and Portia.
2. A monkey.
3. Hell.
Exam Practice
Answers could focus on Lorenzo's praise of Jessica ('For she is wise'), her motives for eloping, how they defy convention, audience sympathies for them as lovers, Jessica's conversion to Christianity, Tubal's reports of their behaviour, their arrival at Belmont, their banter and the mood created at the beginning of Act 5. Analysis might include Lorenzo's use of hyperbole,

the significance of their use of disguise, comparisons with Portia and Bassanio, violent exclamations used by Shylock about Jessica and the significance of their references to classical lovers.

Pages 38–39
Quick Test
1. Show mercy to Antonio.
2. Hercules.
3. He thinks he should get what he deserves (i.e. Portia).
Exam Practice
Answers might focus on his status as the ruler of Venice, his role in the court, his sympathy with Antonio and attempt to persuade Shylock to show mercy and his decisions at the end of the scene. Analysis might include his function as a representative of the state and of justice, his negative diction when he describes Shylock, the use of adjectives such as 'stony' and 'inhuman', the contrast in his language to Shylock, his neutrality once the trial has started, his silence through most of the scene and his use of questions and imperatives, reflecting his authority.

Pages 40–41
Quick Test
1. Salerio and Solanio.
2. Shylock and Bassanio.
3. He (Launcelot) has died.
Exam Practice
Answers might focus on his expected role as a clown or fool, his employment by Shylock and Bassanio, his role as a go-between, his meeting with his father, the trick he plays on his father, how their relationship compares to Jessica and Shylock's, the use of the metaphor 'my very staff', and his relationship with Jessica and Lorenzo. Analysis might include the significance of his name, his references to the Bible, his use of the word 'devil' to describe Shylock, his 'chop logic' and word play, the potential for visual comedy and his interaction with the audience.

Pages 42–43
Quick Test
1. Shylock, Jessica and Tubal.
2. Salerio and Solanio.
3. Aliens (foreigners).
Exam Practice
Answers might focus on Antonio's treatment of Shylock, Gratiano's taunting of him, Salerio and Solanio's attitude to him or Launcelot Gobbo's language and attitude. Analysis might include Salerio's use of alliteration, connecting 'daughter' and 'ducats', the use of animal imagery such as 'dog', 'cur' and 'wolvish', how Shylock is addressed as 'Jew' and the juxtaposition of derogatory adjectives with 'Jew', Shylock's direct address to those he considers anti-semitic', Antonio's justification of his hatred of Shylock and Launcelot's use of the word 'devil'.

Pages 44–45
Quick Test
1. The synagogue.
2. By marrying a Christian (Lorenzo)/becoming a Christian.
3. The fact that he is a clown or fool.

nswers might focus on his need to deal with Christians, his
eeling that they are hypocrites, his use of Biblical references
o insult them, his warning to Jessica about 'Christian fools'
nd his being invited to dinner by Bassanio. Analysis could
nclude his use of rhetorical questions and **parallel phrasing**
o compare Jews and Christians, the implications of his
omparison of Bassanio to the prodigal son and his statement
hat he hates Antonio because he is a Christian, mirroring
ntonio's hatred of him because he is a Jew.

ages 46–47

uick Test

.   By marrying a Jew (Jessica).
.   She is sexually attracted to Bassanio.
.   They happen before the end of the play.

xam Practice

nswers could focus on Portia's lack of choice in the historical
ontext, Bassanio's mixed motives, their love for each other,
essica and Lorenzo's marriage in defiance of convention
nd Portia and Nerissa's testing of their husbands. Analysis
night include both Portia and Bassanio's use of images to
o with power, the symbolism of rings (including the ring
essica swaps for a monkey), the significance of eyes, Portia's
ersonification of love, the use of words such as 'blood' and
ecstasy' to suggest sexual attraction and the significance of
he couples mentioned by Lorenzo and Jessica in Act 5.

ages 48–49

uick Test

.   They need to borrow money from them to engage
    in trade.
.   Profit made honestly/taking care of money sensibly.
.   By choosing it he shows he is not interested in wealth
    but choosing it makes him rich.

xam Practice

nswers might include the centrality of money and trade
o the plot, different attitudes to borrowing money,
assanio's lack of money and desire to marry into it, Portia's
nherited wealth, Shylock's love of money, Jessica's stealing
of money and then waste of it and Shylock's rejection of
money in favour of revenge. Analysis could include Shylock's
uxtaposition of 'thrift' and 'blessing', his use of metaphor
house'), the visual impact of the three caskets, Shylock's
eeing things in terms of numbers and frequent references to
ucats, the double meaning of 'fortune' and the irony of the
nan who chooses the lead casket becoming wealthy.

ages 50–51

uick Test

.   She appears to act as legal adviser, judge and prosecutor.
.   By forgiving sins.
.   By not having Shylock killed and by charging him a fine
    instead of taking half of all his property.

xam Practice

nswers might focus on Shylock's refusal of the Duke and
assanio's requests to show mercy, Portia's speech about
mercy, mercy seen as an important Christian idea, the Duke's
mercy shown to Shylock, whether the Duke and Antonio do
how mercy and Portia's forgiveness of Bassanio. Analysis

might include the simile used to describe mercy, the repetition
of the word, the example given of rulers as people who
should have mercy, religious language, the reference to the
Lord's Prayer and her command to Shylock to 'beg mercy'.

Pages 52–53

Quick Test

1. Go to Shylock's house to help Lorenzo and Jessica
    to elope.
2. Foolish/arrogant.
3. His love for Portia.

Exam Practice

Answers could focus on the use of the masque, Jessica's
disguise as a page boy, Portia and Nerissa's disguises and the
contexts of Elizabethan theatre and gender roles. Analysis
might include the use of dramatic irony, the comedic
confusion caused by Portia and Nerissa's rings being given
to 'men', how characters use disguise to reveal their true
selves, Portia's use of sexual innuendo, how Morocco and
Bassanio draw morals from their choice of casket, and how
cross-dressing might cause audiences to question traditional
gender roles.

Pages 54–55

Quick Test

1. By leaving instruction about how her husband will
    be chosen.
2. Her swapping of the turquoise ring for a monkey.
3. He cannot see what his daughter is planning.

Exam Practice

Answers might focus on relationships between Portia and
her father, Shylock and Jessica, the Gobbos, and Antonio and
Bassanio. Analysis might include Shylock's images of a dead
Jessica, the implications of Jessica valuing her father's ring less
than a monkey, parallels between old Gobbo and Shylock, the
difference made by Portia's father being 'holy', Launcelot's
ideas about 'the sins of the fathers', and Jessica's reference to
her 'heinous sin', visual comedy of mistaken identity between
the Gobbos and Antonio's giving of his flesh for Bassanio
recalling a parent/child relationship.

Pages 60–61

Quick Test

1. Understanding of the whole text, specific analysis and
    terminology, awareness of the relevance of context, a
    well-structured essay and accurate writing.
2. Planning focuses your thoughts and allows you to
    produce a well-structured essay.
3. Quotations give you more opportunities to do specific
    AO2 analysis.

Exam Practice

Ideas from the extract might include the following: Shylock's
pleasure at having Antonio ask to borrow from him; his
sarcastic tone and possible impersonation of Antonio;
repetition of 'moneys'; reference to Antonio's physical attack
on him; use of rhetorical questions; the way he develops
Antonio's derogatory image of him as a dog; the impact of
the short line (implying a long pause) 'Say this'; his sarcastic
version of himself acting as a stereotypical 'humble' Jew;
Antonio's unapologetic, provocative response.

Answers

Ideas from the rest of the play might include the following: Shylock's later repetition of Antonio's treatment of him in an angry and emotional speech; personal dislike based on differences about lending money; dislike based on prejudice; Antonio's actions clearly based on anti-Semitism; in response Shylock says he hates Christians; Shylock's pleasure in Antonio's misfortune, putting revenge before money; his refusal to show mercy; Antonio's response to being asked to show mercy.

Pages 64–65 and 72–73
Exam Practice
Use the mark scheme below to self-assess your strengths and weaknesses. Work up from the bottom, putting a tick by things you have fully accomplished, a ½ by skills that are in place but need securing and underlining areas that need particular development. The estimated grade boundaries are included so you can assess your progress towards your target grade.

Pages 68–69
Quick Test
1. Understanding of the whole text, specific analysis and terminology, awareness of the relevance of context, a well-structured essay and accurate writing.

2. Planning focusses your thoughts and allows you to produce a well-structured essay.
3. Quotations give you more opportunities to do specific AO2 analysis.
Exam Practice
Ideas from the extract might include the following: Shylock's use of prose, exclamations and repetition, showing his excitement and distress at losing money; his focus on money rather than Jessica; his precise knowledge of what he has lost; his reference to 'our nation', reflecting stereotypical ideas about Jews; his shocking images of Jessica in her coffin; use of parallel phrasing; use of minor sentences, showing emotion; reference to Jessica as a thief, implying she is a stranger because of her actions.

Ideas from the rest of the play might include the following: reliance of Venice on trade; plot based on a financial transaction; Bassanio and other Christians' careless attitude to money; Portia's wealth; the imagery of the caskets; wealth ultimately being less important to Shylock than revenge; punishment of Shylock seen in terms of fines and property.

Grade	AO1 (12 marks)	AO2 (12 marks)	AO3 (6 marks)	AO4 (4 marks)
6–7+	A convincing, well-structured essay that answers the question fully. Quotations and references are well chosen and integrated into sentences. The response covers the whole play.	Analysis of the full range of Shakespeare's methods. Thorough exploration of the effects of these methods. Accurate range of subject terminology.	Exploration is linked to specific aspects of the play's contexts to show a detailed understanding.	Consistent high level of accuracy. Vocabulary and sentences are used to make ideas clear and precise.
4–5	A clear essay that always focusses on the exam question. Quotations and references support ideas effectively. The response refers to different points in the play.	Explanation of Shakespeare's different methods. Clear understanding of the effects of these methods. Accurate use of subject terminology.	References to relevant aspects of context to show clear understanding.	Good level of accuracy. Vocabulary and sentences help to keep ideas clear.
2–3	The essay has some good ideas that are mostly relevant. Some quotations and references are used to support ideas.	Identification of some methods used by Shakespeare to convey meaning. Some subject terminology.	Some awareness of how ideas in the play link to context.	Reasonable level of accuracy. Errors do not get in the way of the essay making sense.